Boiling the IT Frog:
How to Make Your Business Information Technology *Wildly* Successful Without Having to Learn Anything Technical

Harwell Thrasher

For permissions and questions, please contact the publisher by e-mail at ITfrog@makingITclear.com. Visit http://www.makingITclear.com for other related information about IT, including a subscription to a free monthly e-mail newsletter.

Printed in the United States of America.

Library of Congress Control Number: 2007923635

ISBN: 978-1-4196-6415-1

Table of Contents

Boiling the IT Frog:
How to Make Your Business Information Technology *Wildly* Successful Without Having to Learn Anything Technical

Introduction: We're Off to See the Wizard

Pulling Back the Curtain

There's a scene in the movie *The Wizard of Oz* where Dorothy and her companions are appealing to the Wizard to grant their requests. Things aren't going too well; Oz doesn't want to listen, and he keeps frightening them with flames and smoke. But then Dorothy's dog Toto grabs hold of the curtain behind the Wizard and pulls it open to reveal Professor Marvel working the controls. The professor tries to cover up, and the Wizard utters the famous line, "Pay no attention to that man behind the curtain." Dorothy discovers that the "great and powerful Oz" is just a man using some gadgets, but that in the end he can be quite friendly and helpful.

Technology — and in particular Information Technology — is a lot like the Wizard of Oz. It's impressive, it seems to work miracles, but in the end it's just a bunch of gadgets being controlled by some people just like you and me. Those people can be friendly and helpful, but only if you learn the "secrets" that keep us from understanding what Information Technology (IT) is all about.

This book reveals forty-four of those secrets. I'm going to pull back the curtain and explain the hidden issues that IT organizations have to face on a day-to-day basis. Once you understand these secrets, it will be a lot easier for you as a non-technical person to communicate with someone in an IT organization. And if you're an IT person reading this book, then you'll find it easier to explain things to your customers.

Who Should Read This Book

This book is for everyone who is frustrated with information technology, and every non-technical person who is at the mercy of a seemingly uncooperative IT organization. It's for people who manage IT, people who want to manage IT, and people who wish they could figure out how IT can be managed. It's for non-technical people who want to better understand IT, and it's for IT people who want to better understand why their jobs are so difficult and unappreciated.

Every manager, executive and knowledge worker in today's world uses information systems, and most of these people have a relationship — good or bad — with some part of an information technology organization. This book is for you if you want to improve the relationship between the IT organization and the rest of the company. It's also for you if you just want to improve your *own* IT relationship.

This is *not* a technical book.

I'm not going to talk about bits and bytes and the various parts of a computer. Instead, this is a book about people, their limitations in coping with technology, and how they can better deal with those limitations.

You might be interested in knowing how this book came about. The book is based on a presentation I originally developed in 2003 for the Executive MBA program at the University of Georgia's

Terry College of Business. The Executive MBA program supplements its normal curriculum by bringing in "real world" speakers from the areas of study, and I joined the group to talk about Information Technology.

When I was preparing to speak to the group, I thought about what I've learned about IT over the years I've been in the field, and it occurred to me that a lot of what I've learned can't be found in any book I've ever seen. In particular, there are myths and misunderstandings associated with IT that make it very confusing and hard to manage for someone outside the IT field. I decided to focus the presentation on these areas that are frequently misunderstood by business people.

I ended up with a list of six lessons, and I've expanded on those lessons in this book.

How to Get the Most Value from this Book

Please read Chapter 1 first. After reading that chapter, you can read the book from front to back in the conventional way, or feel free to jump around in the book to read the sections that deal with problems you're facing right now. However, since a number of the other chapters refer to things learned in Chapter 1, it would be best to read that chapter before the others.

At the end of each chapter, you'll find some exercises called "Making IT Personal." These are not the usual exercises you'll find in textbooks. They're not a test of how well you understand the material; they're intended to help you apply the material and make Information Technology more effective in your own business. I encourage you to work on the exercises together with others in your company or organization. This is a book that encourages communication, so communicate as much as possible while doing the exercises.

Exercises — Making IT Personal

1. Before reading the rest of the book, make a quick list of the good points and bad points of the relationship between your business people and your Information Technology organization. When you've finished reading the book, take another look at your list and see if the book has helped you deal with the bad points, and helped you make the good points even better.

2. How would you like to improve your company's use of Information Technology? Write down a few ideas, and see if any of the ideas are supported or refuted by the book.

Chapter 1: Poof, There It Is!

Magic in IT isn't a Good Thing

One of my favorite quotations is from Arthur C. Clarke, "Any sufficiently advanced technology is indistinguishable from magic." The quotation is important because I believe that most misunderstanding about technology comes from the line that we cross when a technology becomes so magical that it can no longer be understood by normal people.

Magic has a mystical language, full of strange utterances and spells, and IT has the same sort of language, full of mysterious phrases like n-tier architecture, real-time response, cooperative processing, and two-phased commit; strange words like firewall, parallelism, and functionality; and acronyms like ERP, CRM, CICS, DMZ, RAID, SOAP and SQL. Is it any wonder that business people get confused? They begin to think they should hire an interpreter just to understand what their own people are saying.

Secret 1: Technology that crosses the line into magic leads to unreasonable trust, illogical thinking, and inappropriate wizardry.

With magic we expect the impossible, and so it is with technology as well. Most of us don't understand *how* the technology works when we're able to talk into a cell phone and engage someone on the other side of the world in conversation, but we take it for granted that it *will* work. And because the ease of a transcontinental phone call seems so impossible, it's not a big leap to expect something more technically challenging without understanding why the challenge is so great.

When something is magic, we don't expect it to follow logic, and we don't apply our common sense. That can be a bad thing when it interferes with our ability to run a business.

Unreasonable Trust

Let's take a few examples of magic from my own experience. Back in the 1970's, I developed the Material Requirements Planning (MRP) system used in manufacturing plants by Digital Equipment Corporation (DEC). The DEC MRP system took the schedule of computers to be built and used a computerized "Bill of Materials" (like a recipe that tells you how to build each computer) to calculate the demand for each part needed to manufacture those computers. The MRP process is complex, but it's relatively straightforward and understandable. The math is done the same way you would figure things out manually, multiplying the demand for a specific computer by the number of components needed in the computer, and subtracting the inventory that's already on hand to create a report that tells the manufacturing people how many of each part to order.

But at DEC it got more complex because people wanted to apply the latest theories from inventory control. Some college professors had determined that there are various formulas for determining the optimum quantity of a part to order. Some formulas are simple, like always ordering in hundreds. Other formulas are extremely complex, taking into account the weighted average of past orders in conjunction with the weighted average of forecasts of upcoming demand.

Our MRP system at DEC allowed the production managers of each manufacturing plant to choose the way that the order quantity is calculated for each item. When we looked at the result of using various order quantity calculations in different plants, we saw something interesting. When the more complicated calculations were used, it was more likely that an error in the order quantity would go unnoticed. So an erroneous MRP order for more than a year's supply might go through unchecked because the people doing the ordering would figure that the confusing calculation was just the computer doing the best thing for the company.

To say this another way, when the function of software is understood by its users, then the users are likely to "sanity check" the result and catch any error. But once the software has gotten so complicated that the process is no longer understood by the users, then the software has crossed the line into magic, and the users develop an unreasonable trust in the system. At this point the users of a system lose their accountability. If something goes wrong, then the error is blamed on the computer, because no one understands how the computer has calculated the result.

Illogical thinking

A few years ago someone gave me a DVD for Christmas, but it was in the wrong format; I like the wide-screen version, and this was narrow screen. I took it back to Best Buy to exchange it, and I encountered a problem. Although most people would regard the two different versions of the same DVD as an even exchange, the Best Buy computer had been set up to treat the two versions as two entirely different stock numbers. And because my gift DVD had been purchased on sale at a price below the current price, the Best Buy clerk insisted that he could credit me with the sale price, but that since it wasn't an exchange for the same item, he would have to charge me for the difference between the credit and the current price of the "different" DVD.

After several appeals to various levels of management, I finally got my DVD without an additional charge, but this is another example of magic. In this case the "magic" of the system is dictating the policies of the store, even though the computer system is leading those policies to an illogical conclusion. Of course it's a system design error; there ought to be a way to treat two different item numbers as equivalent for exchange purposes. But more important is the fact that the clerk insisted on following the system, even when it made no sense. The clerk was unwilling to even consider that the computer could be wrong. Magic led to illogical thinking.

The Attraction of Wizardry

Back in the 1990's I was flying on Delta Air Lines, and I had to change a ticket at the airport reservation desk. It was a relatively simple change from one flight to another. But my ticket was discounted, and a different fare basis had to be taken into account to determine an additional charge.

At that time Delta had an older system in which the reservation agent had to type commands into the computer and then wait to see the result. So as I stood patiently at the counter, the agent typed command after command, occasionally pausing when the computer had an unreasonably long delay. About five minutes later, I mentioned to the agent during one of the delays, "I'll bet you're looking forward to when Delta replaces this system with something easier to use, aren't you?" The answer astonished me, "No, actually I've spent a lot of time getting good at this system; people look up to me, and I would hate to see a change."

The reservation agent had fallen into the wizardry trap. She was now a wizard, and so she was unreasonably committed to keeping the system the way it was, even though it offered low productivity to the rest of the employees, particularly the non-wizards.

Secret 2: New technology always disappoints before it succeeds.

Gartner is a leading technology advice firm; it's a lot like *Consumer Reports*, but it focuses on corporate information technology. Gartner has found that new technologies go through what they call a "Hype Cycle" (see Figure 1). When a new technology is first introduced, everyone has high hopes, and expectations rise on the impact that this new technology will have on business and on the world at large. But invariably, at what Gartner calls the "Peak of Inflated Expectations," the bubble bursts, and reports of real-world difficulties in implementing the new technology begin to drag down people's opinions. These early implementation issues cloud the public perception of the technology, and the reputation of the new technology declines until the hype cycle reaches

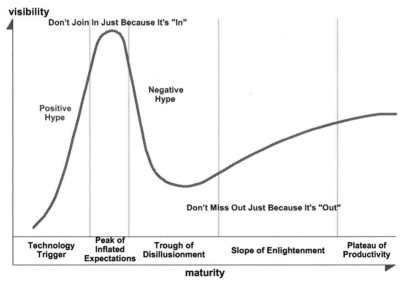

Source: Gartner "Understanding Gartner's Hype Cycles, 2005" by Jackie Fenn and Alexander Linden (June 2005)

Figure 1: Gartner's Hype Curve

a "Trough of Disillusionment." Then, as businesses overcome the initial setbacks and begin to achieve positive results with the new technology, the perception slowly improves, although never to the level that the technology achieved at the "Peak of Inflated Expectations."

Different Aspects of Magic

We've seen two different aspects of magic. In the first, magic systems make people give up their common sense. They trust the system even when the system does things that aren't consistent with reasonable human behavior. And they fall into the wizardry trap, becoming experts in arcane systems and then glorifying their expertise instead of working to make the system easier to use.

Gartner's Hype Cycle points out a second aspect of magic. People have inflated hopes for new technologies, somehow expecting them to do more than they can deliver. Ultimately the new technologies deliver benefits, but not before going through a cycle of inflated expectations.

The lesson to be learned from all this is that technology is *not* magic, but that overly complicated systems give the illusion that magical things are happening. You don't necessarily have to understand a technology to use it, but it helps to have a basic understanding of the principles involved. No one expects a car to fly, because we all understand the idea of an engine pushing a device on wheels. Similarly, if the basic principles underlying an information technology are fully explained, then false expectations can be prevented.

At DEC we ultimately overcame the problem of the magic MRP system by training all of the system users using a paper simulation of the system. We would make up a simple example computer to build, and we would have the trainees fill out worksheets to calculate the number of parts that would be ordered. Then we would have the trainees fill in blank MRP reports to show what the resulting reports would look like. In this way, the system users began to understand that the system isn't magic; it's just doing what they could do manually, but on a much larger scale. The key lesson that we taught is that common sense isn't something to be left behind when using the MRP system; it's something to apply to the new system in a different way.

In the Best Buy DVD example, the cause of the problem wasn't the clerk; it was the system designer who failed to take into account the need for an "even exchange" policy on two different item numbers. The Best Buy clerks were following the rules as they had been taught, and were caught up in a conflict between the computerized company policy and common sense. Not all stores fall into this trap. Some stores like Nordstrom have specific policies which say that common sense always wins out over stupid rules. Nordstrom recognizes that a satisfied customer is more important than blindly following the occasional case where a policy makes no sense. No system, however well designed, is perfect, especially in a changing world, and processes have to be designed to accommodate situations where the system leads to an irrational result.

As for the Delta "wizard," I've often wondered what happened to her. Delta replaced the system she was using, and she lost her wizard status. Or maybe she just started over on the new system and requalified as a new type of wizard. Be careful of wizards within your own company. They often prevent your business from moving forward with changes that are important to your future because they have a psychological commitment to the status quo.

The bottom line from this chapter is to stay grounded and be skeptical. There is no magic in IT except the magic we create for ourselves.

Exercises — Making IT Personal

Use the following techniques to reduce the magic in your own use of IT:

1. Do a "magic audit." Go through all your systems — or at least the key ones — and ask the system users to explain:
a. Where system results come from,
b. How they know that the results are right or wrong, and
c. What happens to the data they enter.

If the system users can't give correct answers, then you need to do better training. And in some cases, you may need to revise your systems to make things easier to use.

For example, in a customer service call center system, the data that customer service reps see on their screens might come from orders entered by salespeople, from records of previous calls, and from information that has been updated directly by the customer. Other data, like a customer credit rating, might be calculated based on the history of orders, payments and returns by the customer. It's important to understand what data comes from where, and how it's calculated, so that appropriate action can be taken to correct bad information. In no case should the customer service reps have an attitude of "it's in the computer, so it must be right." They must understand that the computer system is doing the same things that they would do manually — just doing them faster.

It's also important for people to understand that they are the source of data that feeds other systems. If the consequences of entering bad data aren't made clear, then bad data is going to be introduced into your systems. Here's an example from my experience. A new sales order system was installed which required salespeople to enter various information about the customer along with the order, including annual revenue, number of employees and other high-level descriptive information. Because the use of this data wasn't explained, and because the salespeople weren't properly motivated to gather and enter the data correctly, the salespeople took shortcuts and just guessed at the data they didn't know. As a result, marketing statistics on new customers were wrong, and new ad campaigns were targeted incorrectly.

2. Look at your company's policies for situations where one of your computer systems tells a customer-facing person to do something that's not the best thing for the customer. Does the customer-facing person have the capability to do the right thing anyway? How often does the situation arise? Should the policy be changed?

3. Take a "wizard inventory." Just go up to a sample of people who use a certain system and ask "Who do you go to when you have a really difficult problem with this system?" Then take it to the next level, and ask the identified first-level wizards the same question. By following this approach, you'll identify a hierarchy of wizards for the particular system in question.

Now, here's the key question: how are these wizards (especially the higher-level wizards) involved in the design of system enhancements or replacement systems? There are three possible answers:

a. The wizards aren't involved at all. In this case, you're in big trouble, because your IT organization is in a battle against your wizards. Take steps immediately to find out why this is happening, and intervene to get wizard participation in the process.

b. The wizards are in charge of system enhancements and replacement systems. This can be good or bad, depending on the wizards. If the wizards are resisting process changes and arbitrarily trying to keep everything looking the same as the existing system, then you've got a problem. But if the wizards are looking at the bigger picture and trying to come up with better processes for accomplishing the work, then you're in good shape.

c. An answer somewhere between "a" and "b." The best solution is a partnership of the wizards, the IT organization and — if you have one — a process improvement organization. The wizards supply the knowledge of the existing system, the IT organization provides the tools, and a process improvement organization provides expertise in changing the processes to make them better.

4. Identify the hype cycle stage of the technologies that your company is implementing. Specifically, you want to identify the technologies you're using that haven't yet reached the trough of disillusionment. If you find that you're using any of these technologies, then ask yourself the following questions:

a. Why are you using these unproven technologies? Is it required by a customer? Are you using the new technology to gain competitive advantage? Is there a *really* good reason? If there isn't a good reason, then are there less risky alternatives? Have these less risky alternatives been seriously considered?

b. Is the riskiness of the unproven technology factored into its project plan? Is extra time, money and other resource included in the plan? What's the outcome if the technology doesn't live up to its expectations? Is the potential return from using the unproven technology worth the risk?

After answering these questions, you may still end up using the technology, but you'll be doing so with your eyes wide open.

Chapter 2: In IT We Trust?

Without Trust, IT is Useless

Secret 3: Information Technology is all about infrastructure, projects, maintenance, strategy, and trust.

Your first reaction in seeing this list may be to think that some important things are missing: where's the technology? But just as the subject of cars is not primarily about cylinder heads and spark plugs, information technology is not primarily about software, hardware, networks and systems. Those things are necessary for information technology to work, but you don't need to know *how* those things work in order to make more effective use of IT. In fact, our misplaced focus on the *tools* of information technology has created a much more complicated view of IT than we need. I want you to see a simpler view that is more conducive to a *business understanding* of Information Technology. And in that simpler view, all you have to understand is infrastructure, projects, maintenance strategy, and trust. The other stuff is underneath, but it's not the primary business focus of Information Technology.

In the next six chapters I'm going to talk about each one of the first four elements — infrastructure (in two chapters), projects (in two chapters), maintenance and strategy — and I'll reveal some secrets about each one. Right now, however, let's talk about trust, the fifth element of Information Technology that makes the other four elements possible.

Before reading any farther, answer this question:

- If you're not in Information Technology, do you trust the people in the IT department with whom you work?

- If you're in IT, do you trust the business people with whom you work on a day-to-day basis?

If you answered "yes," then congratulations! Your IT organization must already be dealing with some of the secrets revealed in this book. But please continue reading; there may still be a few secrets that haven't been revealed, and maybe you can increase the trust even more.

If you answered "no" or even "sometimes," then we've got a lot of work to do.

Secret 4: If your company doesn't have a mutually trusting relationship with its IT organization, then IT won't be successful.

An Information Technology organization can be compared to a group of doctors. Doctors have extensive training in very specialized areas, and yet their customers (their patients) don't have any of that training. Doctors have to offer advice every day to patients who don't really understand the details behind the advice. The patient must trust the doctor, since there's no way for the patient to instantly learn all of the factors that influence the advice. Surveys have shown that patients rate doctors higher for their communication skills than they do for their technical ability, and this seems intuitively correct. We can't really tell whether a doctor is technically competent, but we know whether or not the doctor can do a good job of communicating the choices and helping us make a medical decision. Doctors who communicate well are considered better doctors. And the same can be said for IT people: IT people who can communicate well with business people are considered to be better and more trusted.

In certain respects, of course, the comparison between a medical doctor and an IT professional is totally inappropriate. A medical doctor receives much more comprehensive training than the typical IT professional, and the doctor is dealing every day with life and death issues. However, in a way this dealing with life and death issues makes it easier for the medical doctor to offer advice. The usual goal of a medical procedure is to extend the life of the patient or to restore some physical capability that has been taken away from the patient by disease or trauma. The goals of an IT project are usually much more vague. Almost every IT project is aimed at doing something positive for the company, but it's difficult to understand and communicate the IT trade-offs that have to be made among various alternative approaches to achieving the same business goal. Miscommunication leads to distrust, and when you distrust someone's motives, your natural reaction is to ask for a better explanation. The more the IT person explains, the more confused you get. And eventually, if you're like most people, you just give up and go with what the IT person tells you, even though you have a lingering suspicion that you've been hoodwinked. This is not a good basis for future trust.

Why do most of us seem to trust doctors and distrust IT people? I've already mentioned one reason: we start out with the same goal as the doctor — to prolong life or restore physical capability — but we don't automatically share goals with the IT people. Here are some other reasons why doctors are trusted more than IT people:

- Doctors are certified, so we believe that the medical education process weeds out the bad doctors. There is no widely accepted certification process for IT people.

- Medicine appears less complicated than information technology. Medicine is actually more complicated than IT, but we don't usually get very deeply involved in the details of medical science, and so medicine seems simpler. Information technology, on the other hand, is in a state where technical details are constantly being bandied about in the press, usually in a detrimental fashion. We hear enough of the complexity to think that things are more complex than they really are.
- Doctors are trained to discuss medical issues with patients without going into great detail about the problem or the treatment. IT people usually get no training whatsoever in how to discuss an IT problem or issue with a business person. They often try to explain the detail, and they usually just make things worse. (More about this in Chapter 10 when I talk about Simplicity)
- Doctors have a better public image. They're praised for saving people in impossible situations, and even when they fail they're lauded for their extreme efforts. IT people, on the other hand, have the reputation of being geeks who want to play with technology for its own sake. Any time IT people want to spend money on technology, you get the feeling that it's really the technology itself that they want — not something that will benefit the company. IT people who do their job well are usually invisible, but the news media will jump at reporting any mistakes that are made.
- Doctors are perceived as being higher paid than IT people (although the increasing cost of medical malpractice insurance is invalidating this statement). With higher pay comes higher respect, at least to some people. Higher respect brings higher trust.
- Doctors are considered to be honest. They often have to deliver bad news, and they try to be diplomatic and caring, but they still deliver the news, whether good or bad. IT people want to be honest too, but in many cases they get caught up in the detail and don't clearly communicate, so they sometimes

come across as if they're holding back on the truth. Honesty is a cornerstone to trust.

For all of these reasons, IT people tend to be regarded more like auto mechanics than doctors. We know they can fix things, but we secretly believe that they're charging us for more work than we actually need, and at a price that we can't really afford.

But when it comes right down to it, IT people are not trusted because they haven't taken all of the steps necessary to earn your trust. What IT people need to do is to:

1. Take a lesson from doctors on how to communicate. Clarify common objectives. Describe plans in simple terms. Show how recommendations will meet or exceed business objectives. Be clear about risks, but explain how risks will be mitigated. Show sympathy for the needs and concerns of the customer.

2. Under-promise and over-deliver. Be conservative in estimates of time, resource, performance, and benefit. Then do better than the estimates.

3. Be consistent, and be perceived as consistent. If a project that seems comparable to another is going to take longer or cost more, then explain how this project is not comparable at all. If you make a commitment, then honor it.

4. Think like a customer. Try to understand the way customers would look at an IT problem or project, and do what they would want done.

5. Communicate, communicate, communicate. Provide regular updates on the status of work being done. Be honest if things are going badly, but explain what you're doing to make things better. If things are going well, make sure to publicize that situation, but don't say that a project will beat original estimates until it's absolutely certain.

On the other hand, business people need to take a lesson from the way we communicate with doctors. We focus on the results, the costs and hazards of various alternatives, and the probability of success using different approaches. Where it's important to us, we try to understand some of the medical science involved (e.g., the consequences of living with only one kidney), but we don't try to tell the doctors how to do their job.

IT people appreciate the same communication approach from their customers. Focus on the results and the process changes that you would like to achieve. If you have ideas on a solution, then bring them up (just like we bring up treatment alternatives with doctors), but recognize that those ideas may not be applicable in this situation, and the IT experts will understand that and tell you.

One last piece of advice for business people: you wouldn't try to tell a surgeon how to operate, so don't over-specify an IT solution. People who try to be too specific with system requirements get exactly what they asked for, but not what they need.

Exercises — Making IT Personal

1. Do a "trust assessment." Get an independent third-party to do a quick survey on the level of trust that exists between your IT organization and its customers. The third-party doesn't have to be external to your company; it just has to be someone who has no stake in the outcome of the survey.

Take steps to increase trust (see the additional exercises below), but periodically repeat the trust assessment survey to see if progress has been made.

2. Increase the trust between your IT organization and its customers. Part of trust comes from respect and consistent performance, so if the performance of your IT organization has been poor, then this will be difficult. The best way to increase trust in a poorly performing IT organization is to have the IT organization acknowledge its failures and be open about the steps being taken to make things better. You can gain trust even in a failing organization if you're consistent in making progress toward improvement. You don't expect a baby to be a marathon runner, but you

can take pride in the baby's first steps. It's the same with building trust in a failing IT organization: focus on the first steps, and learn to trust the people in the IT organization who are trying to improve things.

Here are some other steps to take:

- Encourage more informal communication between IT people and their customers. Sponsor social events in which IT people are put into non-work related situations with their customers, so they can get to know them better.
- Have your IT people do more "walking around" in the user areas of the building. Let them be visible in situations where they aren't solving problems or delivering news.
- Encourage your IT employees to be trained and certified in their area of expertise. You'll trust them more, and it will increase their capabilities and their self-assurance.
- If it makes sense in your business, have each IT person work in a business job for a day (or just watch) to get a better perspective on user needs and frustrations.

For more on how to deal with IT people, see Chapter 13.

Chapter 3: The Stuff Inside Your Walls

IT Infrastructure

Now let's follow the advice from the previous chapter and explain IT infrastructure in simple terms.

Secret 5: IT infrastructure is just like the stuff inside the walls of your house.

IT Infrastructure includes computers, software, and the networks that connect the computers together. There are hundreds of terms for all of the different types of computers, software and networks, but everything boils down to computers, software and networks, and in most cases you really don't have to know any more than that.

Compare this infrastructure to the infrastructure of your house, which includes electrical wiring, plumbing, telephone lines, cable or satellite TV, heating and air ducts, and the various devices that make all of these things work: furnaces, air conditioners, humidifiers and dehumidifiers, transformers, satellite dishes, etc.

The fundamental issues in infrastructure — both in IT and in your home — relate to keeping the infrastructure working and making sure that it's properly sized for your needs. If all goes well, infrastructure is invisible; it just does its job without attracting any attention. However, there are some secrets to more effective IT infrastructure.

Secret 6: There is no "right" amount of money to spend on IT infrastructure.

This comes as a shock to many people, who take that home infrastructure analogy too far. There does seem to be a right amount of money to spend on home infrastructure, but that's because the infrastructure has become so standardized that most home contractors build houses the same way. There are variations, of course, that are usually associated with the amount of money spent on the overall house. High-end homes are more likely to require additional money for security systems, central vacuum systems, intercoms, and multiple heating and air conditioning zones. But generally there isn't much variation in the amount of money spent on home infrastructure within homes in a given price range.

But suppose for a moment that we were more concerned with risk in our homes. Suppose that our bodies couldn't cope with a temperature range that varied by more than a degree, and that we absolutely couldn't survive for more than a few minutes without electricity or running water. How would that affect the infrastructure cost of our homes?

With higher risk, we would undoubtedly spend more on backup systems. If losing electricity is life-threatening, then we would install backup generators. If losing our water supply is dangerous, then we would drill a well in the backyard and have a pump that could provide an alternative source of water. If a small temperature variation could kill us, then we would buy expensive thermostats, and we would have backup furnaces and air conditioning units in case the primary units fail.

This is radical thinking for a home infrastructure, because almost no one has problems this extreme, but infrastructure risk is a common subject for business. Businesses have created the expectation for their customers that the business infrastructure will always be available to perform the work that is required. Customers can order goods over the Internet twenty-four hours a day, seven days a week. Any outage will not only create a lack of trust, it will probably result in the customer's business going elsewhere.

Fundamentally, the amount of money that a company needs to spend on IT infrastructure is directly related to the company's tolerance for risk. In my home infrastructure example, our cost goes up when we decide that certain things aren't good enough. If we can't survive without electricity, then we need to spend money on a generator. The same thing applies to IT infrastructure; electrical outages can disable computers and prevent a company from delivering its goods and services. Additionally, a lot of IT infrastructure cost is spent on avoiding sporadic problems. Additional network capacity is purchased to deal with the delays that occur during occasional peak usage. Server capacity is also sized for these periods of peak usage, with redundant servers available in case other servers fail during these peaks.

If you're willing to tolerate some occasional delays and outages, then your infrastructure costs will be dramatically lower. Small companies know this very well, because:

1. They usually choose to invest their limited funds in areas other than infrastructure, in an effort to maximize the return from their investment.
2. They minimize their investment in infrastructure by sharing resources wherever possible.
3. They figure that extraordinary personal efforts can usually be applied to work around most of the occasional glitches.
4. They don't have much of a customer base, so their outages don't inconvenience very many people.
5. They're usually privately held, so they only have to answer to a small number of investors.

As companies get larger, however, their tolerance for risk declines, and their IT infrastructure costs tend to go up as a percentage of their revenues. Larger companies have larger cash reserves, and are more visible as targets for lawsuits. Their customer base grows, and so the impact of a failure becomes more newsworthy. And the companies usually go public, and have to answer to investors who don't understand (or care about) the probability of certain risks. All of these factors make larger companies more risk averse, and so their infrastructure cost rises.

What's amazing, however, is that the large companies tend to forget about their higher infrastructure costs. Then they're shocked when they buy a small company in the hope of leveraging the apparent huge profitability of the small company. What the large companies usually find is that some of that profitability disappears when the infrastructure of the smaller company is upgraded to the lower-risk standards of the larger company.

Secret 7: Almost any software and hardware will work in the short term, but you'll see the difference in the long term.

Let me explain by talking about cars. Everyone seems to have an opinion about the best and worst cars. You'll find people who won't drive anything unless it comes from Germany, and others who insist that Japanese cars are more reliable. There are those who insist on buying an American car, and those who prefer something made in Italy. But let's be honest here; won't all of these cars take you to the store and back? Yes, different cars will offer varying levels of comfort. And yes, some of the cars will attract more attention from the people you pass along the way. But all cars are fully capable of moving people from one place to another.

Hardware and software are very much like cars. There are people who swear by Microsoft products and others who swear at them. There are those who only want to use Open Source products like Linux (where the program code is shared and maintained by many different organizations), and others who want a single vendor for everything. But all software products in a given category will pretty much perform the basic function for which they've been created.

It's important to understand this for two reasons. First, because you will have people swear to you that they can only live with XYZ product, and I want you to know that it's a lie; they don't have to get XYZ product. Second, because you won't be able to tell in the short-term whether one product is better or worse than another product; it's only in the long-term that you'll see a difference. And when I say long-term, I mean long enough that it's likely that a mistake won't be noticed until the person making the product decision has moved on to another job, at which point his or her successor might discover the problem.

"I can't live without XYZ"

Let me start by explaining why people feel that they can't live without XYZ product. In most cases they make the statement because they've already used XYZ product in the past, either with a former employer or on their own, and they're comfortable with the product. They may have developed wizard status in the product (see Chapter 1 on magic), but wizard status isn't necessary for them to want to stay with a product with which they're familiar. It's human nature to want to minimize change, and if they're used to working with a product, and if they've been successful with the product in the past, then they're going to want to work with it again.

In some cases people say that they can't live without XYZ product because they've been taken in by the product hype (see Chapter 1 on the Gartner Hype Cycle). If you can't seem to do your job quite as well as you would like, it's human nature to want to believe that there is an outside "magical" solution that will solve your problem. Airline magazines are particularly good at oversimplifying things to the point where it appears that merely buying a product will give you immediate benefit. Magazines are also good at hyping a product to the point where it becomes a status symbol; you get the feeling that your company is nothing unless you have an XYZ system. This is the IT equivalent of keeping up with the Joneses.

Now objectively, we know that we ought to use rational criteria for making buying decisions, and that we ought to consider factors such as these:

Factors in a Rational Product Buying Decision
Functionality of the product (What does it do? How does it do it?)
Vendor viability (Will the vendor survive? Will the product be supported and maintained the way we need? Will the vendor upgrade the product to support future standard platforms? Will the vendor continue to be a leader in their field?)
Availability of skilled talent in the use of the product (employees, consultants, trainers)
Suitability of the product to your company's current environment and to your evolving needs
Ease of integration or interface of the product with your other infrastructure
Amount of change required to migrate from a previous product or platform (in dollars, in training time, in learning curve, in obsolescence)
Cost of the product, both for the initial purchase or license as well as for ongoing maintenance, support and training

These factors are obviously important, but do any of these factors matter to the person who "can't live without XYZ product"? No, because there is an *emotional* basis to their desire for the product, and emotion outweighs rational thought almost every time. Even when we go through the process of rationally comparing alternatives in a decision matrix, we usually start out with an emotional bias toward one of the alternatives, and we often find ourselves weighting the criteria so that the "rational" choice matches our emotional choice. In effect we cheat to build a pseudo-rational justification for our emotional bias.

Yes, emotion outweighs rational thought, but rank outweighs emotion. If the person who can't live without XYZ product is at a low level in the company, then for many companies the answer is pretty simple; say "no" and force the person through the bureaucracy of presenting a rational case for the product. It's all done very diplomatically, with words like "I can understand why you might want the product, but you'll have to put together a proposal to show us why we should follow your advice."

On the other hand, if the person who can't live without XYZ product is at a high level in the company, then there's a very good chance that the company will move to acquire XYZ product whether or not there's a true rational case to be made for it, because a pseudo-rational case will be constructed to justify the decision. Emotion and rank together outweigh virtually everything.

You won't see the difference in the short-term

OK, so the company gets XYZ product. What happens next? There is a flurry of activity as various people assigned to the implementation of XYZ product put their best efforts into getting the product installed. Processes are changed, people are trained, and XYZ is put into action.

Initially, things get a little bit worse, and then they get better. This is almost always true. Things get a little bit worse because there's a learning curve associated with any new product, and productivity declines at least a little bit as users of a new product adjust to the new way of doing things. Then things get better because the product users get through the learning curve and so their productivity picks up. And almost always, their productivity will be higher than it was before the implementation of XYZ product.

With the increase in productivity, the proponents of XYZ product declare victory. "See," they say, "I told you that XYZ product would help our company." But they have failed to take into account the Hawthorne effect, which provides a short-term improvement from almost any change.

Back in the 1920's, an experiment was done at the Western Electric Hawthorne manufacturing facility in Cicero, Illinois. Experimenters wanted to see if higher illumination levels would increase productivity among the plant workers. Sure enough, as the lighting level was increased, productivity among the workers went up. The lighting level was increased again, and productivity went up some more. Then, as a validation, the experimenters decreased the lighting level, expecting that productivity would go down. Instead, when the lighting level was decreased, productivity went up even more.

The experimenters discovered that it was the interest they were showing in the workers that was increasing productivity levels — not the changes in the lighting. And since that experiment, the term "Hawthorne effect" has been applied to situations where productivity goes up due to increased attention paid to workers.

Let's go back to our XYZ product example. The Hawthorne effect pretty much guarantees that almost any change in a process will have *some* positive effects in the short-term. And indeed, the emotional reasons that justified the product in the first place will carry some weight during the product's initial use. But in the longer-term, knowledge of the previously ignored negative aspects of the product will emerge, while responsibility for the initial acquisition of the product will be forgotten. The original advocate for the product will move on to other interests and maybe other companies, and the product will become just another part of the IT infrastructure. Responsibility for the product will move to the IT organization, and if the product was an inappropriate choice, it will become just another contribution to IT ineffectiveness.

Secret 8: The fewer Information Technology products you have, the better off you'll be, as long as you've chosen good products.

IT products are like factories which process data to make it into more usable information. If you're in the manufacturing business then you need at least one factory (or access to one that belongs to someone else), but you don't necessarily want more than one. A few hundred years ago it was common to build factories wherever there were large groups of consumers — high shipping costs and long transportation times made it a necessity. These days transportation costs are much lower, and it's even common to build your products on the other side of the world. In today's world, fewer factories are needed.

There are a lot of disadvantages of having multiple factories, and many of the same disadvantages apply to IT platforms. Every factory requires its own capital equipment, its own maintenance staff, its own production engineers and its own workers. It's the same with IT products. Each product requires its own set of experts in the particular technology being used, so the more products you have, the more experts you need.

Multiple factories make it more difficult to achieve large economies of scale. If there's idle time in one factory, you often can't shift production from another factory that's experiencing peak demand. It's the same with IT products; idle time on one type of computer or idle time for one type of engineer can't easily be used to handle high demand for another product. And the fact that you distribute your systems demand across multiple products means that you can't get the same volume discounts from your vendors that you could if you used only one product.

Now consider various IT products and their differences from the user perspective. Let's start with computers and their operating systems. The interface for a "green screen" mainframe system (no mouse, heavy reliance on function keys on the keyboard) is very different from the user interface to Microsoft Windows (in which the mouse is the primary interface tool), and there are even fairly substantial differences between the user interfaces for Microsoft Windows and the Apple Macintosh Operating System, which both use a mouse.

When you get above the operating system level, there is even more variation. There are radical differences in the way that users relate to various software packages for Customer Relationship Management (CRM) and Enterprise Resource Planning (ERP), and any application developed internally within a company is likely to have a user interface that is totally unique to that company.

What should be clear by now is that fewer products are better. You probably knew that intuitively, but you may not have understood exactly how much better it can be for an organization to have fewer products. Here are some of the types of costs associated with having multiple products:

- Higher cost for the hardware and software because you can't get the same volume discount with multiple vendors that you do with a single vendor, and because you have to keep more hardware and software maintained and up-to-date
- Less opportunity to share best practices across the company
- Less opportunity to share data and information across the company (e.g., have you ever received a word processing document that requires a product you don't have on your computer?)
- Training issues when you transfer an employee from one location to another
- Time wasted on a continuing basis as the employees who favor one product argue with the employees who favor another product

- Greater difficulty in getting technical support coverage from the IT employees who have to be available around the clock to handle emergencies. The more products you have, the harder it is for the IT employees to be expert on all of the products.
- Greater difficulty in sharing databases among the various systems and products (Have you ever tried to pull together data that is stored in two different databases in two different but very similar systems?)
- Difficulty in buying or building new products which need to integrate with the existing systems of the company

OK, so if it's obvious that fewer products are better, then why do most companies have far more hardware and software products than they should? Here are some of the reasons:

- Initial product choice decisions were made differently in different parts of a company
- A company grew through acquisition or merger, and the systems in the new part of the company run on a different type of computer or operating system
- A senior executive couldn't live without product XYZ (see Secret 7 in this chapter), and product XYZ only runs on a nonstandard operating system or computer.
- A salesperson convinced the company that product XYZ is required (again, see Secret 7 in this chapter).

Now, before I leave this secret, I want to go back to the last phrase in the secret, "as long as you've chosen good products." This little phrase is the real gotcha in product choices, because it's impossible to know exactly how technology will evolve over time, and how successful your vendors will be. You might pick a product like the IBM mainframe and be satisfied for a lot of years, or you might pick one of the hardware vendors who are no longer with us. Hardware vendor names like Burroughs, Univac, NCR, Control Data, Honeywell, Data General, Digital Equipment, Wang, and Compaq come to mind. All of these companies were considered to be "safe" computer choices since they were leaders in the computer field, but none of these companies sell their own computers today.

Some people advocate going with multiple products just as a way to cover your bets and ensure that some of your systems will survive. For hardware products, I don't agree with this philosophy at all. Many of the older hardware vendors, including the first eight in my list, had proprietary operating systems, and so the cost of losing a hardware vendor was much higher since you would lose an operating system as well. That's not nearly as true today. Most vendors have standardized on some version of Unix or Linux, or the hardware vendor supports Microsoft Windows, so even if a hardware vendor goes away, the migration to a new hardware vendor isn't as difficult as it once was.

For operating systems like Unix or Microsoft Windows, I also don't see the need for multiple platforms just for safety. Various versions of Unix and Linux are widely supported by many companies, so I don't see much risk there. Microsoft is in theory a single vendor risk, but it's such a big company that I don't see any real danger in support going away for its current products. Even if Microsoft as a company went away, there are enough users of Microsoft software for someone to step in and support the users who are left behind.

For applications software, especially third-party software like Customer Relationship Management (CRM) or Enterprise Resource Planning (ERP), there is some clear vendor instability due to ongoing mergers and acquisitions in the software industry. But frankly, CRM and ERP are too big an investment in the processes of your company to deliberately go with two vendors. It's tough enough to successfully install CRM or ERP for one vendor; I can't imagine deliberately going with two.

Exercises — Making IT Personal

1. Is there any IT project currently going on (or proposed) in your company that sounds like one of the "I can't live without XYZ" projects that I described in the chapter? Is there a real rational case that can be made for the project (see Chapter 5 on picking projects) or is the case for the project mostly based on emotion? If it's based on emotion then:
- Should the project continue?
- What can be done to prevent projects like this from being started in the future?

2. Do a product inventory. Make a list of the major hardware, operating system, and application products that are being used in your company. Identify areas where multiple products are being used for the same purpose.
- In areas where there are multiple products, is only one of the products "active"? An active product is one that is still being purchased for new employees, or it can be a "platform" (like Windows or Linux) on which new products are being built or purchased. If you have multiple active products in an area, ask yourself why. Are there technical reasons or are the reasons political or wizardry? Is there a way to make only one product active and phase out the others?
- An "inactive" product has no new product activity, new copies are no longer being purchased, and it is only being maintained for the people who already use it. For inactive products, evaluate the cost of migrating the remaining users of that product to an active product versus the continuing cost of maintaining the system where it is.

Chapter 4: Keeping the Pipes Clean

Optimizing your IT Infrastructure

For most people, the software side of infrastructure is particularly hard to understand because of the intangible qualities of software, and because of the confusion between software and business processes. Chapters 7 and 10 will address some of the intangible aspects of software. In this chapter, I'll describe some of the secrets of software and its impact on business processes.

Secret 9: Keeping software users up-to-date on current versions is much more difficult than you'd think.

Have you ever seen a plate spinning act in which the performer spins a plate on the end of a stick, and then gradually adds more and more plates to more and more sticks until there are twenty or thirty plates spinning simultaneously? When performers doing this act get to their limits, they're running furiously from plate to plate, trying to keep the old plates spinning while trying to start up new plates. It's a frantic performance.

Keeping software up-to-date is a similar process. Software providers usually release one or two updates per year for each software package, and in many cases there are interim updates to patch bugs and to protect against newly discovered security threats. Most of this software runs on multiple computers in your company, and you probably have mobile or home users so that the computers aren't even in the same location at any point in time. Obviously, updating every computer with every software release is a large effort.

Each software release requires a critical decision: how soon does the software update have to be installed? Caution dictates that you don't want to be one of the first customers to update your software — it's better to let others find the problems in the new release. But when there are security threats to be prevented, the decision gets more difficult. The announcement of the release has notified the public that a vulnerability has been detected, and like bees swarming around a flower garden, hackers will immediately start trying to exploit the vulnerability and breach your security. Companies which delay implementing the patch are more likely to be hacked.

But wait — it gets worse. Although software vendors claim to test their software with all of the most popular combinations of hardware and other software, there are too many combinations to make the tests 100% reliable (and of course the software vendors *never* test their new release against your custom adaptations to their software or against your company-written software). Any update to any software package might cause another software package to stop working.

Compounding the problem is the arrival of new computers for new people or for new purposes. New computers are designed and tested with the latest versions of software products, and so the new computers may arrive with different software versions than the ones already in use in your company.

Worst of all, software releases make assumptions about the revision levels of prerequisite software to be found on your computer. So a seemingly trivial but important update to package A might require an update to package B, which might in turn require an update to package C, and so on.

Infrastructure managers have to find the right compromise between highly conflicting goals. On the one hand, they want to have everyone in the company using the same version of software so that support issues are minimized, so that people can easily interchange data with one another, and so that best practices can be shared. On the other hand, the infrastructure managers know how difficult it is to test new versions of software with the combinations of software and hardware that are used in the company, and how hard it is to roll-out software upgrades to the large number of distributed computers.

Some infrastructure managers try to develop a limited number of standard configurations, and to keep all of a certain type of user on the same configuration. So, for example, sales reps might use a certain model notebook PC with a standard set of applications at the same release level. Updates to the configuration are delayed as long as possible, and then the combination of new software versions is tested before updating all of the sales rep computers.

With PC's, there is an additional challenge to keep personal software like video games off of the computers. It's not, as many people think, because the company doesn't want you to waste time on personal software. It's because the personal software can cause problems with the business software already on the PC. In effect, it tinkers with the standard configuration.

There are a few things you can do to help infrastructure managers with the thankless task of keeping computers up-to-date:

1. Respect their wishes and leave the computer hardware and software configuration alone. If you start monkeying with the configuration or if you upgrade software or install new software on your own, then you're going to make it more difficult for the business software to work, and you're going to make it extremely difficult for the infrastructure group to support you.

2. When the infrastructure managers want to delay implementation of a new software release for a while after it comes out, try to understand that they're acting in your best interests.

3. Follow Infrastructure Secret 8, and minimize the number of software packages that are required. Every software package introduces another variable in the system testing that is performed before software is updated in your company. And it creates unnecessary redundancy to use multiple software packages for the same purpose in different parts of the company.

Secret 10: If you're going to use off-the-shelf software, then use the business processes that come with it. Otherwise you're just paving the cow paths.

Off-the-shelf software is great, but the biggest mistake people make is trying to force the system to follow their existing business processes, rather than to use the processes already included in the system. The more expensive the software is, the bigger the mistake can be.

When I lived in Boston, I heard the story that the streets in downtown Boston were never planned, but that instead the city fathers took the easier approach of putting roads where cows had worn paths in the former grazing land. Essentially they "paved the cow paths."

Whether the story is true or not, the situation fits many companies who buy off-the-shelf software. Rather than to plan for its most efficient use based on the business processes that come with the software, the company continues their old way of doing things, and attempts to apply the new technology (the software) to their old processes.

With smaller software purchases — things like word processors and spreadsheets — there isn't a lot of opportunity for product customization, and so most people learn to live with the software the way it is. But with larger software purchases, like a Customer Relationship Management (CRM) system, a Sales Management System (SMS) or an Enterprise Resource Planning (ERP) system, the software is designed to be customized, and so most companies take advantage of that design and do a large amount of customization. The price of this customization can exceed the cost of the software itself many times over.

Let's use Enterprise Resource Planning (ERP) as an example. It's an expensive set of software from a company like SAP or Oracle that is supposed to be an "off-the-shelf" solution to many of your company's problems. It typically includes software to do accounting functions like general ledger, accounts payable, accounts receivable, billing, and payroll, and some specialty functions like manufacturing and distribution for those companies that need them. It also includes Human Resources (HR) software to track employee information, and it frequently includes elements of a Customer Resource Management (CRM) system: things like customer tracking, call center, marketing, etc. Companies buy ERP systems because the inner workings of most companies are pretty similar. You might manufacture a different product, or you might distribute something different from everyone else. You might have a service you offer that's different from other companies. But underneath it all, there are a lot of common processes that are shared by most companies. It doesn't make economic sense for your company to write specialized software for most of your company's needs any more than it makes sense for you to construct your own car from scratch. Just buy the software that is the best fit for your needs, and then adapt your processes to fit the ones that come with the software.

It sounds reasonable, but that's not what most companies do. Most companies start out in that direction, creating a list of their requirements and then matching up ERP software with their requirements to find the best fit. But after the software is purchased, that's when the problems begin.

If you were used to riding a bicycle, would you buy a car and then replace the steering wheel with handlebars and replace the brake pedal with hand-brake levers? No, you'd learn how to drive the car the way it was designed to be driven. But most companies buy ERP software and then try to adapt the software to the processes they were using in their company *before* the software was acquired. And because many of these process changes turn the software upside down, like trying to steer a car with handlebars, the software never ends up working as well as it should, and the old processes aren't ever really implemented the way you wanted them to be.

Why do people insist on trying to force fit their old processes into their new system? Some of this goes back to the wizardry issue I mentioned in the first chapter; people who are wizards at your current processes don't want to switch to new ones because they'll lose their wizard status. And some of the issue is just human nature and inertia; people naturally resist change. But I've seen companies waste millions of dollars and years of effort in trying to have a new ERP system do things it was never designed to do. Some of these efforts even result in the entire new system being scrapped.

Take my advice. If you're going to invest in an ERP system, or in any major system that will change the way your company works, make it clear to the system's users in advance that you're first going to implement the system "as is" and follow the processes that the system is designed to use. If you still need to fine-tune things after a year or so, then go ahead. But be very sure that any alteration to the system is absolutely essential. Make sure you differentiate between a reason (why you are a certain way) and an excuse (why you stay that way).

Secret 11: The biggest revolution in Information Technology in years is in the area of middleware, integration broker technology, and web services.

These words, "middleware," "integration broker," and "web services," are probably new to you, and they sound typically geeky, combining words you know into something that sounds magical (back to that magic again). So let me explain this in English. In business we typically don't have just one software package that does everything for us, in spite of what the ERP package vendors are trying to sell us (see Secret 10 for more on ERP). For example, we might buy one software package for Human Resources and another for General Ledger, use an outside payroll service, and do customer management using some software that was written inside our company. Then we might use the manufacturing part of an ERP system like SAP for inventory control and order processing, but use an outside service for sales leads.

Even though these different "applications" were purchased as standalone systems, there is a need to move data back and forth among the applications. Sales leads should flow into the customer management system and the order processing system. The inventory and order processing systems should feed accounting data into General Ledger. And all of the systems should get their employee lists from the Human Resources system.

It would be wonderful if all of these systems would use the same database, but it's not likely. Most off-the-shelf software requires its own dedicated database. But at the same time, most systems rely on data that originates in another system. If that data can't be obtained electronically, then it has to be reentered manually from one system to another. Obviously we would prefer an electronic connection, and it should be timely so that each system can count on the most up-to-date data available.

The traditional way to address the data interchange problem is to design the systems to put out periodic feeds from one system to another, and to periodically load data from other systems. But each feed between two systems has to be hand-crafted to fit the specific data in the source and destination systems, and then these hand-crafted feeds have to be kept up-to-date as the systems change.

The problem grows geometrically with multiple systems. Two systems require only two feeds (A to B and B to A). Three systems require six feeds (A to B, B to A, B to C, C to B, C to A, and A to C). Four systems require twelve feeds. Five systems require twenty feeds. By the time you get to ten systems, you need ninety feeds, and you need 380 feeds by the time you get to twenty systems. The more systems you have, the worse the problem gets.

Now picture a different approach. Instead of connecting each pair of systems together with feeds, let's assume we have some new piece of software that acts as an intermediary among the various systems, like the service that FedEx provides: you give them the package, and FedEx makes sure it gets to the right place. How many connections do you need? With two systems, you need four connections: A to the connector, B to the connector, the connector to A, and the connector to B. With three systems, you need six connections, one from each system to the connector, and one from the connector to each system. And as you add more systems, the number of connections doesn't increase geometrically like before — it's simply the number of systems times 2. So twenty systems requires just 40 connections — not 380 feeds.

This approach, using an intermediate piece of software to interconnect your systems, goes by various names in the technology world. Some vendors call it "middleware" because it sits in the middle between your systems. Some vendors call it an "integration broker" because it acts as a broker among your systems to integrate them together. And you'll also hear the phrase "web services" because some of this software uses a specific way of communicating with the systems called "web services."

Regardless of what it's called, this technology is a breakthrough in information technology. For the first time it is possible to interconnect all of your systems without all of the hassle, cost and overhead that have been associated with the traditional system-to-system feeds. When successfully used, it will revolutionize IT infrastructure and provide a way for your business to interconnect all of its systems so that the pace of your business can increase, and so that you can begin to look at your company data in a whole new way.

Exercises — Making IT Personal

1. Who decides in your company which software updates are to be installed and when they are to be installed? Is the person (or organization) doing a good job? How well do other people in your company understand the criteria for the decision? Is the person (or organization) appreciated, or is the person the butt of company jokes?

2. Think about the process that has been used in your company for installing off-the-shelf software. If you've installed a major software package like CRM or ERP, what percentage of your total package expense has been spent on adapting the off-the-shelf software for your company's specific needs? It's not unusual to spend many times more on the adaptation than on the software itself, but it's not always money well spent.

3. Is your company using middleware, integration broker technology or web services? If so, then find out more about how this technology is being used in your company, and how you can support the effort. If the technology is not being used in your company, then find out why.

Chapter 5: Think of a Number Between 1 and 1,000

Picking the Right Projects

Projects are the second element of Information Technology. Projects make it possible for things to change within your IT infrastructure. It is not a requirement that you have any IT projects within your company, but I don't know of any company without them.

Secret 12: A key to successful IT projects is selecting the right projects to do. A bad project selection process will lead you to the wrong projects.

IT projects are selected in most companies using one of two approaches, or a combination of the two. In the first approach, an IT project is chosen because it's required for achieving some major business goal. If the business goal contributes to overall corporate strategy (that is, it's a "worthwhile" goal), then this is a very good reason for selecting the project. This approach follows top-down-strategy thinking; set high-level business goals, then set lower-level goals which contribute to the achievement of higher-level goals.

A second approach for selecting projects is commonly used in companies where high-level business goals have not been set, where the high-level business goals are unclear, or where there are too many conflicting high-level business goals (generally indicative of a lack of focus in the company, and particularly prevalent in larger companies). In the second approach, projects are compared to each other, and a number of the "best" projects are selected to move forward, with the actual number of projects depending on the IT budget.

Of course, it's difficult to compare projects when they are supposed to accomplish so many different things. For example, how do you compare a sales force automation initiative with an improvement in the customer service web site? The answer in most companies is to convert all projects to a common denominator: dollars. This is commonly done by calculating the Return on Investment (ROI) of each project and then comparing the ROI numbers. But there are a number of problems in the ROI calculation, ROI isn't working in most companies, and as a result, businesses are making bad project decisions.

Secret 13: Using Return on Investment (ROI) for project selection is a ticket to failure unless some stringent rules for calculating ROI are put in place.

Let's start with a basic definition for those who aren't familiar with ROI. To calculate the ROI for a project, we need two things: an estimate of the cost of doing the project, and an estimate of the benefit that we'll receive from doing the project. Then these numbers are translated into ROI by various formulas that vary from company to company, and sometimes department to department. Some formulas are complicated and use "discounted cash flow" (thereby potentially causing the "magic" problem — no one really understands what you're measuring), while others are simpler and just divide the benefit accrued during some number of years by the cost over those years. In any case you end up with a number that's a percentage — just like the interest rate being paid by a savings account. One project might have a 15% return on investment and another project might have a 475% return on investment. Then the projects are ranked based on this return, with the higher ROI projects considered better for the company.

The definition seems reasonable, but here are some of the reasons ROI isn't working:

Biased Proposals

In most companies, project proposals are put together by the people who want the projects to be approved. It might be a marketing or operations department who benefits from a project, or it might be the IT group itself. In any case, proposals are going to be deliberately biased to make the projects look good because the people writing the proposals know that they have to compete against other project proposals which are similarly biased toward their own projects. Making projects look good isn't a problem, but when these same people do the ROI analysis for their projects, the results are far from fair and objective. ROI exaggeration becomes a game, and under the rules of this game, if a benefit *can* be claimed, then it *will* be claimed, whether or not there is any probability of it actually occurring, and whether or not it will have real financial benefit to the firm. For example, if a new system has the potential to save an hour per week for 200 secretaries, then you can be sure that the average hourly wage of a secretary (with benefits) will be multiplied by 200 and then by 52 weeks to chalk up some annual financial benefit. Never mind that the hour will probably be absorbed by other tasks, and that no financial savings will actually accrue to the company.

On the other hand, if the secretaries have to be trained on how to use the new system, and if there's a learning curve involved, then you can be sure that this training time will be minimized in the estimate (maybe an hour or less per secretary). In addition, the labor costs associated with people being trained will likely be ignored, and the learning curve will be neglected altogether. The general rule for preparing the ROI in a proposal is to maximize possible benefits and to minimize possible expenses, thus inflating the ROI beyond all reality.

Omission of Secondary Costs

But it gets worse. In their eagerness to get their project approved, the proposal writers will conveniently forget that aspects of their project will increase costs in other areas. This is especially likely if a project resource is shared with other projects or other departments. Things like increased network traffic or server usage will probably be ignored. And even more likely to be forgotten are the tertiary costs such as increased support dollars for those secondary higher resource demands.

Neglect of Transition Issues

Of course, no project will get its full payback on the first day that a new system is installed. Not only will there be a transition period while users learn a new system, but in most cases there will be a short-term decline in productivity and quality while people make mistakes and then figure out how to deal with a new environment. Yet most ROI proposals show only two worlds: the one before the project is implemented, and the vision of the perfect new world after the project is completed. The costs of the transition period are usually ignored.

Minimization of Risk

Risk is usually forgotten in ROI projections. This is particularly ironic since risk is such a large part of project management once a project gets approved. Nevertheless, it is rare that risk is considered in ROI since an ROI projection boils down to one number, not a series of numbers. Have you ever seen an ROI calculation that says, "there is a 50% probability of a $100 million savings, a 40% probability of no savings, and a 10% probability of a $50 million loss"? I doubt it, since ROI proposals usually show only one outcome: the successful one. Any problems with risk are considered "implementation issues" and won't be addressed until the project is started.

Also conveniently omitted from many project proposals is the increased risk to the business of becoming dependent on a new and less reliable process. This is the risk of the new system itself, which is over and above the risk of whether or not the project can be successfully completed.

Missing Prerequisites

Prerequisite projects are often ignored or forgotten when calculating ROI. Sometimes it's an accident; the proposal writer assumes that another project is already approved or under way. Sometimes it's deliberate; a true ROI game player can carefully craft a project with a huge ROI by conveniently pushing some of the costs into separate projects (e.g., infrastructure improvement). Since the process for ranking projects usually only compares projects one at a time, without looking at prerequisite projects, you can get approval for a high ROI project and then "discover," after the fact, that other unapproved projects are required as prerequisites. In most companies, the commitment to the "high ROI" project won't be questioned or reexamined. Instead, the company will grudgingly approve the prerequisites that should have been included in the ROI calculation in the first place. What's the real calculated ROI of the project? We'll probably never know.

No Follow-up Measurement

OK, so the project gets approved. How many companies go back after the project is complete and actually measure the costs and benefits to calculate the real ROI? I've never seen anyone do it (If you have, I'd like to hear about it). And even if the costs and benefits are measured, there's a high likelihood that the numbers will be distorted and therefore unusable. Labor savings are minimized by other process changes that weren't anticipated when the project was proposed. Costs are shared with other projects and so cost accounting is difficult. And underlying volume assumptions have changed — up or down — and this affects the measurement. It's very difficult to say whether the project ROI was actually achieved, and so the proposal writers who inflated the estimates get away with their crime, and they will go on to use similar tactics in additional projects.

Summary - Why ROI isn't Working

ROI isn't working because the highest ROI doesn't go to the best project — it goes to the most creative exaggeration of ROI by a proposal writer. But in spite of its deficiencies, I'm not saying that ROI ought to be discarded as a tool. Next, I'll give you some recommendations for improving the accuracy of your ROI calculations, and for selecting the projects which can provide the most benefit for your company.

How to Improve ROI and your Project Selection Process

So far in this chapter I've explained why ROI isn't working in most businesses. I want to quickly point out that I don't believe that the "game players" I mentioned are bad people, in spite of my use of the word "crime." I believe that everyone falls into that game-playing mentality when confronted with a process that requires it. It's the process that's at fault — not the people. The people just learn that in order to get a project approved, they have to exaggerate the ROI, and this provides the basis for the problem.

So how do we fix the process? The core of the problem is an inherent bias in figuring ROI, so let's try to eliminate the bias. Here are some techniques you can use:

1. Have a single group of people who determine the projected ROI for all projects, or who at least review the ROI calculations for projects to make them consistent. Eliminate the advantage that imaginative exaggerators have in doing project proposals.

2. Ensure that ROI proposals include all costs, including all prerequisite projects, infrastructure requirements, and all secondary and tertiary costs. If a project is to be implemented in phases, then include the ROI for each phase as well as the cumulative ROI for all prior phases, and make sure that it's clear to everyone that a later phase cannot be accomplished without an earlier phase, and therefore cannot be approved without the earlier phases.

3. If a project depends on a prerequisite that is also a prerequisite for other projects, then either (a) break out the costs of the prerequisite that are a specific requirement for this project, and include them in this project's ROI calculation, or (b) go ahead and approve the prerequisite and take its costs out of the ROI calculations for all of the projects on which it depends.

4. Differentiate in proposals between real dollar savings which affect the bottom line and theoretical savings (e.g., an hour

saved per week from each of 200 people) which may be absorbed by the business.

5. Specifically include a section in each proposal on the transition from old system to new: how the transition will occur, how long it will take, what will happen, and how productivity and quality may be impacted during the transition. Factor those productivity and quality costs into the ROI.

6. Include consideration of risk by doing scenario planning in the proposals that require it. Identify the risks in a project, including probabilities of various outcomes. Explicitly identify potential issues, and discuss the steps that will be taken to minimize or eliminate them. Develop multiple ROI calculations based on various likely scenarios, and then build a single composite ROI number based on a probabilistic weighting of the various ROI numbers. For example, if there is a 50% probability of a $100 million savings, a 40% probability of no savings, and a 10% probability of a $50 million loss, then the composite benefit number used for the ROI calculation is $100 x .5 + $0 x .4 - $50 x .1 = $45 million. This may still be a project worth approving, especially if clear steps are taken to minimize the 10% probability of a loss.

7. To the extent possible, go back after each project to determine the actual ROI that resulted from the project. This should be done as part of a generalized project close-out process, which should also discuss things that should be done differently in the next project.

8. Even better, get user commitment for savings before the project starts. For example, if the project is going to eliminate the need for one clerk in each office, then go ahead and reduce the office budgets in advance to reflect the savings. If the project succeeds, then the savings have already been locked in. And now every office has an additional incentive to make the project successful, because they're already committed to the savings.

I've used this last approach successfully in two different companies. In both cases, advance commitment was made to head count reductions in anticipation of savings from a new system. Because the commitment was made far in advance, the companies were able to meet the head count reduction goals through normal attrition without any layoffs. And the system ROI was easily achieved because the savings were built into the budget.

The Missing Project Selection Criterion

By using the techniques listed above, you can reduce the bias in ROI estimates. But consistent ROI estimates aren't enough; an underlying problem with using ROI for project selection is that the project with the best payback isn't always the best thing for your business. Your business has a strategy for advancing in the marketplace, and the best projects are the ones that help implement that strategy — not necessarily the ones with the highest ROI. Choosing projects based on ROI may contribute to the bottom line in the short-term, but this approach will not position your company for the future.

Secret 14: Adding strategic alignment to the project selection process ensures that IT projects move the company in the right direction.

To improve the project selection process, add another criterion to project selection: strategic alignment. There are a lot of ways to do this; here are a few:

a. Use an ROI multiplier. For example, if the project is in strong alignment with the strategic direction, multiply the ROI by 1.5 to get an "adjusted ROI"; if the project is in moderate alignment, use the ROI as is (a multiplier of 1); if the project goes

against strategic direction, then multiply ROI by 1/2 or 1/4. Then rank projects on the resulting adjusted ROI.
b. Use strategic alignment as the primary criterion. Only consider projects that are in strong or moderate alignment with strategic direction, regardless of their project ROI. Kill projects that go against strategic direction.
c. Use strategic alignment as a project budget allocation tool. Set aside a certain amount of the project budget (say, 75%) for projects that are aligned with strategic direction. Then spend up to 25% of your project budget for unaligned projects if their ROI is higher than any aligned project.

You can work out the specifics of how to use strategic alignment in your project selection process; the important thing is that it is taken into consideration in some way in your process, and that the project selection process is kept simple enough to be understandable.

Conclusion - How to Fix ROI

ROI is probably the best known project ranking tool, but it's seldom used consistently and correctly. We're kidding ourselves when we say that we use ROI to rank projects on financial returns. The reality is that calculating project ROI is a game in most companies, and the best game players get their projects approved.

However, you can change the rules of the game to make ROI a better reflection of reality. And you can ensure that your projects are strategic by measuring their alignment with strategic direction. The result will be a better choice of projects for your business, and a higher percentage of successful projects overall.

Exercises — Making IT Personal

1. What approach does your company use for selecting IT projects? A top-down approach or a project-to-project comparison (or a combination of the two)? After reading this chapter, how should the process be changed?

2. Is Return on Investment (ROI) used for project-to-project comparison in your company?
- If not, then what is used instead? Does the method have the same problems that I pointed out for ROI?
- If so, then does your ROI process suffer from the problems I described? What can you do to fix the problems in the use of ROI to compare projects?

3. Is strategic alignment used in your project selection decisions? How is strategic alignment factored into your project selection process?

Chapter 6: You Want It *When*?

Making Projects Successful

According to studies by the Standish Group, only 35% of IT projects started in 2006 were considered successful (completed on time, within budget, and meeting user requirements), and 19% of software projects were abandoned altogether. Those statistics are bad enough, but in fact they represent a great improvement over earlier study results. In 1994 the Standish Group found that only 16% of IT projects were successful, and a huge 31% of software projects were abandoned.

Entire books have been written on how to make projects successful (see the Endnotes for recommendations), but here are some of the secrets that I have discovered from my own experience.

Secret 15: Good project management is asking the right questions.

A project manager's principal job is to ask questions. The process starts when the initial project plan is put together and the project manager asks everyone "What are the steps required?," "How long will each step take?," and "What can go wrong?" After the initial project plan is put together and a project estimate is determined, then the project manager goes back to the plan contributors and asks "How can we do things differently to make this project go faster and smoother, with less risk and less expense?"

After agreement is reached on a revised project plan, the project manager continues to ask questions as progress is made on the plan, but now there are questions like "How can we make up the time we lost on this task?," "How can we take advantage of the time we gained on this other task?," and "How do we rearrange the tasks in the project plan to stay on schedule and under budget?"

If you're outside a project looking in, maybe as a manager or as the recipient of some of the project deliverables, then there are questions you can ask as well. I've found these questions to be the most important:

- Is there a single person responsible and accountable for project success? If not, then the project is less likely to succeed, and any failure will turn into a finger-pointing exercise.
- Does the schedule include time for prototyping? It's best to do a small test of important aspects of the system before investing a lot of money in unproven concepts.
- Does the schedule include time for adequate testing at all levels? It's traditional IT wisdom that the cost to fix a mistake grows by a factor of 10 at every stage of the project. Catching a mistake in design saves the most. Catching the mistake when programming can cost ten times as much to fix. Catching the mistake when system testing can cost one hundred times as much. And catching the mistake after implementation can cost one thousand times as much as finding the problem in design. Obviously it pays to find mistakes as early as possible.
- Does the schedule include time for rework? It's natural to assume that some mistakes will be made, but is there time included in the schedule to fix them?
- Does the schedule include time for user training? Surprisingly, this tends to be a frequent omission if your IT organization is focused on delivering software instead of implementing a business change.

- Is the internal schedule date (the date the project team is shooting for) farther out than the best case estimate? In other words, is there a cushion between the two dates? If the two dates are the same, then your schedule is too aggressive. The best case estimate assumes nothing will go wrong, and that never happens.
- Is the project commitment date (the public date announced for scheduled project completion) farther out than the internal schedule date (the date the project team is shooting for)? These two dates are often the same, but this means that there is no slack in the schedule, and the likelihood of on-time delivery is low.
- Is the project commitment date farther out than the best case estimate? This sounds like a dumb question, but you would be surprised how often these two dates are the same. This means there is absolutely no chance that the project will finish on time, because a "best case" date is never achieved.

Secret 16: All projects have risk. Good projects deal with it, and bad projects just hope for the best.

All projects have risk, whether it's technical risk ("we're not sure this will work"), business risk ("we're not sure how well this will be accepted by our customers"), or financial risk ("we're not sure how much this will cost"). Good project plans explicitly list the risks of the project, together with a contingency plan for each risk and a "trigger event" that will cause the contingency plan to be invoked. When you are presented with a project plan to review, here are some of the questions you ought to be asking about project risk:

- What are the highest risks? What contingency plans are in place for each risk? What is being done to mitigate each risk (make it less likely to happen)?

- At what level in the project plan is "slack time" included? Is there slack at the task level, phase level, or at the level of the overall project? My personal preference is that the slack time be included at the level of the overall project. That's because slack time is generally regarded by the project team as "breather time," a time when everyone can slow down, catch their breath, and prepare to go on to the next part of the project. If slack time is included at the task level, then there will be a breather after each task. If a task is finished early, then the next task in sequence won't be started early; instead the time will be used for a breather. If no task ever starts early, then there's almost no chance that delays caused by a late task will ever be made up, and the result will be a late project. Keeping slack time as a high-level reserve is the best approach, because it keeps the project moving forward aggressively. When a task finishes, the next task starts right away, and there is a possibility that early tasks can make up for any delays caused by late tasks. The slack time can be allocated out to late tasks as needed, but keeping it in reserve until that point is the best way to help a project finish on time.

Secret 17: Most projects fail for the same reasons.

In my own experience, here are the biggest reasons for IT project failure:

1. Starting the wrong project. It's the wrong project when the business doesn't want it or need it, or when it's not the best thing for the business to focus on *right now*. It's also the wrong project if the project solves the right problem but does so using an ineffective solution. If you start the wrong project and discover the error during the project, you might be able to move the project toward the right direction. But the delay is still likely to cause the project to fail. Make sure you're doing the right project *before* you start.

2. Not including prerequisite steps. Unfortunately, it's very common for project proposal writers to conveniently omit project prerequisites when they're trying to sell the project (see Chapter 5). This keeps the estimated project costs down, and it raises the calculated Return on Investment (ROI). If you're lucky, the omitted prerequisites will come to light when the detailed project plan is put together, but if you're unlucky then the omissions won't be caught until the project is already under way. In either case, a blame game will ensue, with business people typically blaming the IT people for forgetting to include things like the need for increased network infrastructure, or a requirement for interfaces to other systems. Sometimes this leads to cost overruns, but it's just as likely to kill the project altogether. Be absolutely sure that all prerequisite projects and costs are included in your initial project estimates.

3. Going for home runs instead of base hits. In baseball it's *runs* that count toward winning the game. It's very satisfying to see someone hit a home run, but the game of baseball is more often won with consistent singles. Projects are the same way. Huge projects are impressive, but they're much more likely to fail. You'll get better results by breaking the large projects into smaller sub-projects, and accomplishing the smaller sub-projects one at a time.

4. Project duration greater than the job tenure of the sponsoring executive. Most successful projects can count on an executive "guardian angel" to fight off enemies and make sure that the project resources are allocated as needed. If the sponsoring executive changes jobs before the project is completed, there is serious risk that the successor in that executive role will be less committed to the project success (for more on this subject, see the description of "stepsystems" in Chapter 12). In fact, it's fairly common to see the project killed just *because* the predecessor executive supported it. Make sure that a project ends before the sponsoring executive disappears. The best way to ensure this is to keep your projects short.

5. "Gathering" requirements instead of *negotiating* them. We hear that phrase "gathering requirements" all the time. It gives the impression that business analysts run around from office to office with pails to collect the requirements like so many blueberries. Often the requirements really are just gathered, with analysts capturing people's suggestions and writing them down, no matter how good or bad they are, and no matter how cost-effective they are. The result is a project that's doomed to failure because these requirements are often full of contradictions and unnecessary distractions.

Let's use an example to show how it works. If I ask a group of people what they want in a car, they will probably list things like economy, high performance, sportiness, aerodynamics, and the ability to carry the entire family plus lots of cargo. Many of these factors are contradictory and take the result in different directions. A car that has room for a large family probably won't be too sporty, and it won't be high performance. The most economical cars are small, low performance, and not very sporty.

Similarly, your systems are likely to have contradictory requirements as well, and the contradictions ought to be negotiated at the start. High performance systems probably require lots of server power, something that may not fit with a requirement for low cost. Systems that are designed for a novice Internet user often can't be full of bell and whistle features.

Systems design is full of trade-offs, and if you don't make the trade-offs up front during the design, they'll be made for you by the people who put together the system. They probably won't be made to your liking, the system will be a poorer fit for its users, and the project is more likely to fail. It's important to negotiate requirements up front — don't just gather them.

6. Not enough contingency planning. Most projects have surprises, and bigger and longer projects have lots of surprises. Contingency planning anticipates possible surprises and prepares alternative ways to deal with the surprises when they happen. Obviously not all surprises can be anticipated; that's why they're

called surprises. But generalized contingency planning can help you deal with various classes of surprise in a way that doesn't endanger the project. Projects without contingency planning, or without enough contingency planning, are more likely to be unsuccessful.

Exercises — Making IT Personal

1. Identify a few key projects in your company or a few projects in which you have a personal interest. Ask the questions included in this chapter under Secrets 15 and 16, and see if you're comfortable with the answers. If you're not comfortable, then take appropriate steps before the project fails.

2. Secret 17 lists six common reasons for project failure. Think about whether any of these failure reasons apply to your projects. If so, then how can you change the projects to make them more likely to succeed?

3. If you're had any recent project failures, then identify the causes of the failures. What could have been done to make the projects succeed? And more importantly, what are you going to do differently on the next project to avoid the same traps?

Chapter 7: It's Not Just Like Tuning Up the Car

Maintenance — Keeping up with Business Change

Maintenance is a necessary part of Information Technology. It's a natural by-product of projects: as projects are completed and new systems are implemented, there is an increasing base of systems that have to be maintained. It's like a farmer who owns a lot of land, some cultivated and some left in its natural state. Uncultivated land requires no maintenance, but as soon as land is cleared and readied for crops, it requires additional work, year after year, to maintain its state as cultivated land.

With IT it's typical to see projects decline over time as a percentage of the total IT budget because maintenance costs (as well as infrastructure costs) increase with every completed project (see Figure 2 on the next page). If the overall budget remains level, then this increasing maintenance cost takes away from the dollars available for new projects, and the percentage of the IT budget spent on new projects will decline. Only by continuing to increase the overall IT budget (or by discontinuing maintenance of older systems) will it be possible to continue the current level of expenditure on new projects.

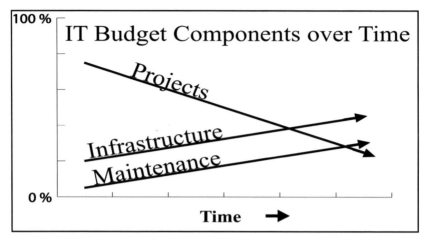

Figure 2

The biggest issue for business people trying to understand IT maintenance is the definition of the word itself. In IT there are two uses of the word "maintenance." Our typical use of the word is the definition that's associated with hardware or machinery, and that's totally different from the definition of software maintenance. Let's take a car as an example. When you drive it off the show-room floor a new car is in as good a condition as it will ever be. From that point forward you'll spend money on car maintenance to try to bring it back to the capabilities it had when it was new. IT maintenance of computer hardware works the same as the car example; maintenance is aimed at keeping hardware running the way it ran when it was new. (See Figure 3).

Secret 18: Software "maintenance" follows different rules from hardware maintenance, and should be planned and budgeted differently.

Software, on the other hand, doesn't wear out or change its behavior due to age; software will continue to do what it was sup-posed to do until the day you stop running it. For software, the

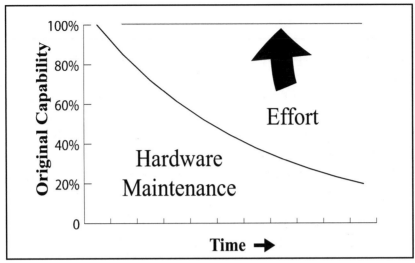

Figure 3

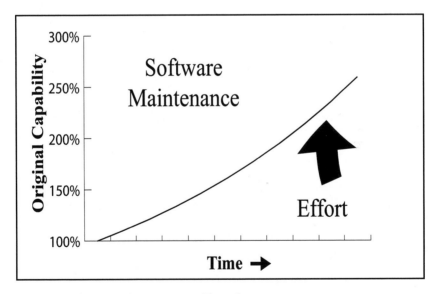

Figure 4

word "maintenance" means something totally different: it means the changes that are made to the software to adapt it to changing business conditions (see Figure 4). For example, if software was written to support a six-digit account number, then it will continue to support a six-digit account number forever. But if the business decides it needs an eight-digit account number, then the software will have to be changed ("maintained") to support the eight-digit number.

Because the two definitions are different, people get confused when they talk about software maintenance. And the element of magic (see Chapter 1) makes it more confusing because non-technical people don't know how to apply common sense to their software maintenance expectations. For example, let's say I'm a twenty-one year old recent college graduate, single and carefree, and I drive a small red two-seater sports car. Then I get married and have a couple of kids, and my requirements change; now I need something that will transport the whole family. Would I expect to take my sports car to the shop and have it "maintained" into a minivan? Obviously not! But almost any business person would expect to "maintain" a single-user homegrown software application into a multi-user system without a second thought. We know from our common sense that a sports car can't be changed into a minivan. But we don't know how to apply common sense when dealing with what's possible or impossible in terms of software changes.

As a direct result of this confusion over the definition of maintenance and our lack of common sense on the subject, we feel like we're at the mercy of the IT organization. But there are no right answers for when software ought to be replaced instead of maintained, just as there are no right answers on the best time to sell a car (or junk it) and buy a new one. The best course of action in dealing with an IT organization over maintenance issues is to:

1. Have your IT organization clarify its software maintenance budget. Now that you know that software doesn't require maintenance to keep doing what it's doing, you might want to question why a certain amount of software maintenance money is allocated for every system, even the older ones. Typically this money is spent on requirements that originate with other systems (like the change in the number of digits in the account number). But often

the users of the older systems continue to tweak things long after the system is working. These users will tell you that the changes are necessary, but push back a bit and see how much money (if any) the changes will save. Sometimes it's best to just cut off maintenance for some systems unless a specific problem in the software needs to be solved.

2. Recognize that the requirement for software maintenance over time is different from the requirement for hardware maintenance. Hardware requires the smallest amount of maintenance when it's new, and the maintenance requirement increases over time as more parts wear out. Software often requires the *highest* amount of maintenance when it's new, because a lot of small problems are being discovered and they need to be fixed. Then the requirement for software maintenance declines over time as most of the problems ("bugs") have been discovered. But as the software reaches the end of its useful life (because your business has changed), you'll see the maintenance requirement rise again. That's when you should begin to consider replacing the system with something that better suits your current business needs.

Exercises — Making IT Personal

1. Before you picked up this book, did you understand that software maintenance means something totally different from the way we normally use the word "maintenance"? How are you going to use your new understanding of what software maintenance is all about?

2. Are there cases where you are trying to "maintain" a system to turn it into something that it's not meant to be? What are you going to do about it?

3. What percentage of your company's overall IT budget is allocated to hardware maintenance? To software maintenance? How

has that percentage changed over the last few years? How has the *actual dollar amount* for hardware and software maintenance changed over the last few years? What conclusions can you draw from these trends?

4. If your company tracks the maintenance cost of specific IT systems, take a look at the history of maintenance costs for the systems that interest you. Is the number for a given system declining every year or increasing? If it's increasing, then is the system getting close to the end of its useful life?

Chapter 8: Are We There Yet?

Creating an IT Strategy

In spite of all of the advances made in technology over the years, there are very few companies who feel that their Information Technology (IT) organizations are making the maximum possible contribution to the business. Although IT organizations usually start with the best interests of the business in mind, somewhere along the line most IT groups fail to reach their full potential. I've talked about some of the reasons in this book; lack of trust, unnecessary complexity, working on the wrong projects, inappropriate management, poor motivation, and more. But regardless of the reasons for prior failures, there is a way for companies to bring their IT organizations back in alignment with business objectives, and to make their businesses more successful through better use of information technology.

Secret 19: An IT organization without an IT strategy is like a sailing ship without a destination; it's anybody's guess where you're going or when you'll get there. But pick a destination, and you'll begin to see progress.

This chapter describes a process that can be used to define an IT strategy that maximizes the benefit of the IT organization, and which positions the IT organization for continued benefits on an ongoing basis. Companies that apply this process will see better payback from their IT investments, and overall improvement in their bottom line.

In Chapter 2, I introduced that idea that IT is infrastructure, projects, maintenance, strategy and trust. In almost all companies we'll see IT infrastructure, projects and maintenance, and we'll often see trust. But not enough companies have an IT strategy. That's a bad thing; it's like sailing a ship without having a destination. Strategy is the least understood aspect of Information Technology, and yet the part of IT with the most payback.

Let me use an analogy. If you think of systems as buildings, then putting those systems in without a strategy is like allowing anyone to put up buildings without any city planning or zoning. You might get a mansion next to a trailer park, adult entertainment next to a church, and houses thrown together without any provision for water, sewer or electricity. City planning puts together an overall plan for a city, and then ensures that the infrastructure is put in place to support the buildings, and that the roads and streets will support the people who live and work in those buildings (I'm not saying that city planning is successful everywhere, but at least there is an attempt).

An IT strategy is like city planning. It starts with business objectives, sets IT policies and principles to support those business objectives, includes standards for hardware and software, adds a "technology architecture" (like a building architecture) that shows how systems will fit together, and ties everything together with an IT plan or road map that shows how the company's systems will progress over time.

An IT strategy is what differentiates average IT from great IT. If your IT organization doesn't have an IT strategy that includes all five of the components mentioned above, you owe it to yourself and your business to create one.

Business Strategy

Let's start at the beginning. The IT organization is part of a business. The business has a purpose and it has existing processes that define the current way that the business operates. The shareholders and directors of the business want to improve the business in certain ways, probably growing revenue and profits, maybe moving into some additional markets, and probably doing some other things that are specific to the business. Therefore the business has objectives — general statements that describe where the business is going and how fast it wants to get there.

A business strategy describes in broad terms how these objectives will be met. The business strategy includes both policies and high-level plans. The policies define fundamental assumptions that employees will use in their day-to-day decision-making — things like the ones in this table:

Sample Business Policies
We manufacture our own products
We sell through distributors
We put honesty and ethical behavior above all else

The high-level plans define a general plan of attack to accomplish each objective. For example:

Sample High-Level Business Plans
We will expand our market share by acquiring one of our competitors

Sample High-Level Business Plans
We will improve our customer service by taking advantage of the latest technology advances in centralized call centers

At this level, strategy is very broad. It deliberately doesn't go into detail about specifics. This is because:

1. There are a lot of details that have to be worked out at lower levels in the organization, and it would be premature to state any assumptions about those details.
2. High-level business objectives are likely to take a long time to achieve (at least months, and possibly years). Therefore it would be a mistake to be too specific; things are likely to change a great deal before the objectives are achieved, and the strategy has to be adaptable to changing conditions.

Information Technology Strategy

Think of strategy as existing at multiple levels in a business. At the highest level, a business sets objectives and develops a strategy to achieve them. Then at each successive lower level in the business organization, a strategy is developed to provide the next level of detail associated with the achievement of the higher level objectives. This is the classic "top down" implementation of strategy within a business.

The IT strategy, then, serves two objectives:

- It fleshes out some of the details omitted from the overall business strategy, saying how some of those business objectives will be accomplished.
- It sets the strategy for the IT organization, thereby providing members of the IT organization with their overall direction, from which they can create successively lower level strategies.

In the best businesses, the strategy setting process isn't strictly top down. At each level of the organization there is feedback that is used to improve the strategy at the level above. This is especially true in IT, where senior business executives may be unaware of the ways that IT can facilitate some potential areas of business improvement until someone in the IT organization tells them.

The best IT executives will not just sit passively back and figure out how to implement the overall business strategy. Instead, they will actively participate in the process to set overall business strategy, making sure that the business objectives take best advantage of opportunities presented by current technology.

Secret 20: The IT organization should actively participate in setting business strategy in order to leverage their technology expertise for maximum business benefit.

Don't just let IT figure out how to implement the business strategy they're given. If you do, then you're not taking advantage of the talents and experience of your IT people. It would be like setting a marketing strategy without any participation from the marketing organization, or determining a sales strategy without help from the sales department. And a business strategy that is developed without IT participation won't be effective, because I can guarantee that some of your competitors will involve their IT people in their own strategy.

The Elements of a good IT Strategy

I'm now going to describe an approach for
- Defining the IT strategy which is best for the business,
- Using the strategy to get IT aligned with business objectives, and then

- Putting processes in place to keep IT aligned with business objectives and making maximum contribution on an ongoing basis.

There are five elements of the IT strategy:

1. The business objectives that will be supported by IT, along with the corresponding IT objectives that show how the business objectives will be accomplished
2. The IT policies (sometimes called principles) that, like the business policies, will define fundamental assumptions that employees will use in their day-to-day decision-making
3. Standards that will be followed
4. The "architecture" that will result from putting together the policies and the standards
5. The plan or "road map" that will define the sequence of things to be done in order to accomplish the objectives

Unfortunately, many IT strategies only include elements #3 and #5. The consequences of this omission will be discussed in more detail later.

Right now, let's go into more detail for each of the five elements.

Element 1. The business objectives that will be supported by IT, along with the corresponding IT objectives that show how the business objectives will be accomplished

Without this fundamental information, the IT organization has no defined purpose other than to "do work as requested." Some IT organizations that omit this element in their strategy actually operate that way; they have project request lists and their "strategy" consists of doing the projects that have been requested.

Think of how successful a company would be if the company opened for business and just did whatever people asked them to do, without any defined business purpose. The company would be good at some things and would be bad at others, due to inexperience, inappropriate tools, or lack of proper guidance. They might make money if they charged enough for their services, but the results of their work would be inconsistent, and no piece of work for one customer would fit together with the work for any other customer. Does your IT organization operate this way? It's not uncommon.

Without a clear focus on business and IT objectives, it's easy to get distracted. It's easy to waste money on projects that don't really contribute to the bottom line, or to spend money on a big project without understanding the consequences of the project implementation to the rest of the business. Obviously, it's important to have objectives in order to focus an IT organization, and to ensure that the IT organization is using the IT business investment to meet the objectives of the business.

Some IT organizations will tell you that they have a list of objectives "in their heads" or somewhere in their files, and that it's not necessary to include the objectives in the IT strategy. I disagree. The IT Strategy should be a complete document that includes all of the context information required for someone to understand not only the direction of the IT organization, but also the reasoning behind that choice of direction. Objectives must be included, or everyone will make different assumptions about the IT direction.

Recap: The first element in the IT strategy is a list of specific business objectives that the IT strategy will support, along with the corresponding IT objectives that show how the business objectives will be accomplished. It is also important that the lists of objectives be prioritized, and that a general time frame be given wherever possible. This is to make it easier to make day-to-day decisions on resource trade-offs that may be necessary among the various objectives.

Element 2. The IT policies (sometimes called principles) that, like the business policies, will define fundamental assumptions that employees will use in their day-to-day decision-making

This element of an IT strategy is probably the one that is omitted most often. Yet IT policies are important because they provide the context in which the IT standards and architecture will be determined. If you don't set policies before you define standards and architecture, then you'll find your organization constantly debating lower-level issues because the higher-level issues are still unresolved.

Earlier in this chapter I included examples of business policies. Here are some examples of IT policies:

Sample IT Policies
Our systems will be available for customer use 24x7. The systems will be secure and reliable, providing protection for our customer and company data.
Our systems will present one face to our customers, with one integrated set of products and systems, accessible over the Internet via one user ID per customer.
We will use a few named standard licensed software packages from third-parties instead of developing software within our company, except where software is required for core products which will differentiate our business from its competition.
We will use a few named standard languages, tools and databases, in order to optimize our development and maintenance costs.

Sample IT Policies
We will remain up-to-date with the technology used within the business, updating software to remain on the current or one-back version, to ensure that we can get vendor support for software.

Recap: The second element in the IT strategy is a set of IT policies that provide the basis for other IT decisions. Develop the policies with participation from both IT and business leaders. Be careful not to have too many IT policies, or you'll dilute their impact on the IT organization — if there are too many, then no one will remember them. The best number is somewhere around ten, but in no case more than twenty.

Element 3. Standards that will be followed

Policies are general, but standards are very specific. The usual set of standards is a list of software and hardware categories, with a set of possible choices for use within each category, and the status of each possible choice. For example, in the category of PC operating system, the choices and their status might be as shown in this table:

PC Operating System	Status
Windows 95	Retired
Windows 98	Retire as PC is replaced
Windows ME	Avoid

PC Operating System	Status
Windows 2000	Retire as PC is replaced
Windows XP Home	Avoid — not for use on corporate LAN
Windows XP Pro SP1	Upgrade to SP2 as part of scheduled maintenance
Windows XP Pro SP2	Standard — order on new PC's until Windows Vista is proven to work with all of our software, at which point Windows Vista becomes the standard for new PC's instead. Do not upgrade Windows XP PC's to Windows Vista.
Windows Vista	Pilot until proven to work with all of our software, then use as standard on all new PC's

A standard can't be as simple as saying "the standard is X" because you need to be able to change the standard over time. By using different status codes, you can address the changes that will inevitably take place in technology. In the example above, the status code "retire" is used for a choice that may have been the standard in the past, but which is no longer the best choice. Nevertheless, the phrase "retire as PC is replaced" is used in recognition of the fact that it may not be cost-effective to upgrade an older PC to the current standard.

Similarly, when a new choice is being phased in, that new choice may be designated as "pilot" until sufficient testing has been done to validate the choice in conjunction with other technologies used in the business. After the validation is done, then the "pilot" status can change to "standard."

It's usually best to list all possible choices, even if they're not recommended. By using a status of "avoid" or "future," you make it clear to anyone reading the standard that the choice has been considered and that the choice is "off limits." If someone in the organization then makes a valid case why there should be an exception to the standard, then add the exception to the list.

In some areas, there may be no standard, but it's still best to list the choices. In such a situation, there may be only exceptions. For example, department A may use choice X and department B may use choice Y.

Although the example uses operating systems, don't restrict your standards to hardware, networks, and system software. Include all of the applications software that anyone in the business may use. For example, include the standard software used by customer service reps and salespeople; for e-mail, calendaring, word processing and spreadsheets; and for every other IT function within the company. The list will be very long, but the length of the list makes the complexity of IT requirements more visible to everyone in the business.

Use the IT policies to help you develop the standards. For example, an IT policy may dictate that you'll use only one hardware platform throughout the company, or that you'll never implement new software until it's been in the field for at least six months.

Recap: The third element in the IT strategy is the list of standards. Use standards to develop an inventory of the hardware and software that the IT organization will support. Base your standards on IT policies.

Element 4. The "architecture" that will result from putting together the policies and the standards

Those outside the information technology area may be unfamiliar with the IT use of the word "architecture." For a building like a house or a skyscraper, the word "architecture" refers to the way that building materials are assembled to form a structure. Similarly, the architecture of an information system refers to the way that software and hardware components are assembled to form the overall system. Just as building architecture has styles, IT architecture has different styles for system construction. Just as building architecture has building codes and best practices to ensure the safety and longevity of a building, IT architecture has system standards and best practices to ensure the security and longevity of a system. And just as building architecture has approaches which make the maintenance and alteration of a building easier and less expensive, IT architecture has approaches which make the maintenance and alteration of software easier and less expensive.

The architecture part of the IT strategy is often omitted, but this omission is a huge mistake. Would you want someone to build a new city without a plan for where the streets should go or how the buildings should look? An IT strategy without an architecture definition is similar — systems would be developed without regard for how they will fit together or even how they should be built to minimize ongoing cost. In an IT organization without an architecture, it's not uncommon to do the equivalent of adding two additional floors to a building which has a foundation that wasn't designed to support the extra floors.

So what does an IT architecture look like? Part of the architecture is better represented by a set of diagrams than by a description in words (For an example of one such diagram, see Figure 5. The specifics of Figure 5 aren't important; what's important is that you have a diagram which shows how your major systems interact around the customer). The diagrams show the various existing

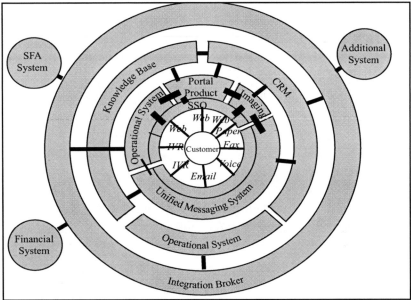

Figure 5 - a sample architecture diagram

systems in the business and how they connect together, sending data back and forth among the various databases. The diagrams should also include future systems (the way that road maps show future highways) so that the reader can understand how the data flows will change in the future.

The diagram speaks to part of the architecture (equivalent to where the "streets" should go), but other parts of the architecture describe the way that systems will be built. The best systems are built of layers and components, and so this aspect of architecture will typically describe the layers and components that will be used, the source of each layer and component (here's where the standards are referenced), and how the layers and components will fit together and interact (For more on layers and components, see Secret 27 in Chapter 11).

The architecture will take into account the IT policies, just as a building architecture takes into account the use of the building. If a system has to be available to users 24x7, then this dictates certain types of architecture. If multiple systems have to be accessible using a single user ID, then this also puts constraints on the type of architecture to be used.

The architecture will also take into account the IT standards. If the intent is to go with a single primary vendor of software tools (e.g., Microsoft or IBM), then the architecture will focus on the way that systems are built using that vendor's tools. If the strategy is to use a major third-party software product (e.g., SAP) as the centerpiece for IT systems, then the architecture will be built around that software product.

Recap: The fourth element in the IT strategy is the architecture that defines the systems requirements for current and future systems, and that shows how systems will be built and modified.

Element 5. The plan or "road map" that will define the sequence of things to be done in order to accomplish the objectives

So far we've included objectives, policies, standards and architecture. There can be a time component to all four of these elements:

- Objectives can have target dates for implementation.
- Policies can reflect a shift from one type of IT approach to another over a designated time period.
- Standards can evolve over time, reflecting the implementation of new technology, or a shift from one vendor to another.
- Architecture can show the current systems and how they'll change or be replaced over time.

The fifth element brings together all of these time-based events into a unified plan. This plan provides cross-references to the other four elements as required, but presents a single time line to make it easy for everyone to understand what happens when. Remember, however, that this time line is at a high-level; we're dealing with projects here — not the individual tasks within the projects.

The plan is more useful if resource assignments are included, at least at a departmental level so that effort and cost can be reconciled against budget. The plan should also show the interdependencies among the various projects in the plan, and should include priorities so that trade-offs can be made when things don't go according to plan.

Recap: The fifth element in the IT strategy is a plan which summarizes all of the changes to be made in a single time line to clearly represent what has to happen, when it should happen, what resource should be used, and how projects are interdependent. The plan should make it clear when business benefit is to be expected from each deliverable.

What does a good IT strategy look like?

By now it should be clear that it is not enough to just have a plan, or even a plan and a set of standards. Like the overall business strategy, the IT strategy is not detailed enough to anticipate every decision and every surprise that the future has in store. Instead, the tools have to be provided to the IT organization to enable them to make decisions that are consistent with the IT strategy, and which help them deal with surprises as they occur.

A good IT strategy provides these tools by including five elements:

1. A specific set of objectives both for the business and for IT, so that the business will know what the target is,
2. A set of policies that can be used as the basis for decisions,
3. A set of standards to be followed,
4. An architecture to show them how to assemble hardware and software components, and to show how systems will fit together, and
5. A plan which shows the desired time line together with the priorities and interdependencies among the projects.

The strategy approach described in this chapter includes all of these elements.

Conclusion

A plan isn't a strategy, although a strategy will lead to plans. Objectives aren't a strategy, although objectives are part of the reason that you put a strategy together. Policies and standards aren't a strategy, but they are definitely needed to implement a strategy. An architecture isn't a strategy, but it describes the vision of what systems will look like.

However, put all five of these elements together, and you can have an IT strategy that:

- Can be understood and followed by both business and IT people
- Can adapt as change is required
- Can best meet the needs of the business by aligning IT effort with business objectives

IT Strategy defines how your IT organization will operate, and serves as the basis for day-to-day decisions. Without an IT strategy, your IT organization is just a ship without a destination, going wherever the wind blows.

Exercises — Making IT Personal

1. Do your IT executives actively participate in the process to set overall business strategy, making sure that the business objectives take best advantage of opportunities presented by current technology?

2. Does your company claim to have an IT strategy? Is it written down? Have you seen it? Is it shared with everyone in the company?

3. Does the IT strategy contain business objectives along with the corresponding IT objectives that show how the business objectives will be accomplished?

4. Does the IT strategy contain policies (sometimes called principles) that define fundamental assumptions that IT employees use in their day-to-day decision-making?

5. Does the IT strategy contain standards, which include a complete list of software and hardware that is in use or will be in use in your company, together with the specific statement of direction for the use of each software and hardware item?

6. Does the IT strategy contain an overview of the architecture of the information systems used in your company, showing how everything fits together into a unified whole?

7. Does the IT strategy contain a plan or "road map" that defines the sequence of things to be done in order to accomplish the IT objectives?

8. If the answer to any one of the first seven questions is "no," then what are you going to do about it?

Chapter 9: Can Nine Women Have a Baby in a Month?

QCSS — Pick Three

There are too many acronyms already in Information Technology, but here's one that you ought to remember. The acronym "QCSS" stands for Quality, Cost, Schedule, and Scope. These are the four dimensions of a project. You build something of a given Scope, it has a certain project Cost, it takes a certain amount of time to do the project (Schedule), and the project is completed with a certain Quality level.

So far, all of this sounds pretty obvious, and yet what most business people don't seem to understand is that there are fixed relationships among the four variables. You can set the values for any three of the four variables, and the value for the fourth undefined variable will be determined by the relationship with the other three variables.

Secret 21: When you define the requirements for a project, you can't specify quality, cost, schedule and scope; only three of the four can be required, and the other variable is dependent on the process being used for the project.

This isn't just true of IT projects; it's true of *any* project. But the magic aspects of IT (see Chapter 1) make it harder for business people to understand these variables for IT projects, and so business people think that the normal rules don't apply to IT projects.

Let's take an example. If you want a system that does a certain thing (Scope) built in a certain amount of time (Schedule), and you expect a certain level of Quality, then you can't specify the Cost; that's the fourth variable that's determined by the other three. If you attempt to specify the cost anyway and your number is too low (the most common situation), then you're putting the project members in a bad position, and they're going to have to come back to you and change one of the other variables. They will probably try to lower Scope (take some of the deliverables out of the system), or change the schedule (push some of the deliverables farther out). They probably won't mention Quality as something that you can change, but if you hold them to Scope, Schedule and Cost, then Quality is the variable that's going to change anyway. You might get your system in the time frame you want and at the cost you want, but its Quality will be low because of the short-cuts the project members have to take (e.g., they'll do less testing).

We use the QCSS principles every day in a non-IT context. If you ask a home construction company for a 3000 square foot house (scope), but you say you want it in 2 months (schedule) at a cost of $50,000 (cost), you realize you'll probably get a pretty crummy house. You know that you get what you pay for, and that speedy construction costs extra. Why should you expect that an IT project will be any different?

Non-Linearity

All of this is complicated enough, but what makes it worse is that the four variables have non-linear relationships. That term may be new to you, so let me give you some examples of non-linear relationships. A woman having a baby has a non-linear relationship among the four variables. One woman can have a baby in nine months, but under no circumstances can nine women have that baby in one month.

Another example might be a group of house painters trying to paint a room. If it takes two painters 8 hours to paint the room, then you might expect four painters to complete the job in 4 hours, and that might be so. But the variable relationships become non-linear if you push things much farther. Can eight painters do the job in 2 hours? Can 16 painters do the job in 1 hour? Can 32 painters do the job in ½ hour? You see what I mean; there comes a point where it's impossible for the painters to do the job without getting in each other's way. The same thing happens with IT projects when you have too many resources working on the project.

Secret 22: Adding more resources to an IT project (especially one that's running late) can make it take longer.

The curve of variable relationships can even reverse (see Figure 6). In our painter example we will probably find that if we put enough painters in the room, then it will take a longer amount

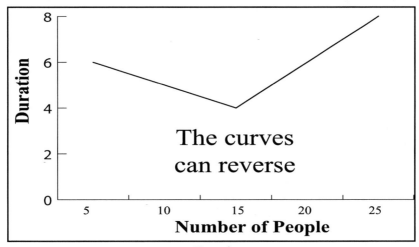

Figure 6

of time to do the job — not shorter. That's because more people require more coordination, and after a certain point it becomes too difficult to split work across multiple people.

This curve reversal happens all the time in IT projects. If an IT project is running late, then there is a tendency for business people to want to add more people to the project to make the project come in earlier. Almost invariably, the project will end up taking even longer, because the new people have to be brought up to speed on what's going on, and tasks can't be easily split among multiple people.

Here's an example of the real-life non-linearity of an IT project (see the table below). In this project the original estimate called for a 13.6 month duration (Schedule) with a peak staff of 6 people and a cost of $416,000. Scope was fixed, and Quality was estimated at 6 defects remaining after the project is complete.

Peak Staff	Schedule (Months)	Cost in $	Estimated Defects
6	13.6	$416,000	6
9	12.3	$623,000	9
14	11.3	$875,000	14
24	10.2	$1,300,000	25
33	9.5	$1,700,000	33
66	8.3	$3,000,000	75

Sample project data

Management wasn't happy with the estimate, and asked the IT group to figure out a way to shorten the Schedule. Scope was fixed, but by adding more people, increasing the Cost, and accepting lower Quality, the project team was able to provide estimates which improved the Schedule. Note that in the last estimate in the chart, the Cost has grown by over 600%, the number of defects has grown more than 1100%, and the Schedule has only declined by about 40%. There is clear non-linearity in the relationship among these variables.

What to do about QCSS?

So what do you do about QCSS? In particular, what should you do *differently*? The main thing is to understand that you only get to specify three of the four variables, and that extreme demands will likely drive the project into non-linear project territory, thereby costing your company a lot of money and increasing the likelihood of project failure. If Cost and Schedule are absolute limitations, then you're better off keeping Quality up and decreasing the Scope of the project.

Your best bet is to do things with high quality in small steps. Specify high Quality and small Scope, and you'll get shorter Schedules and more reasonable Cost. Smaller projects shift the non-linearity curve in the direction that's to your benefit, and you'll be able to do small projects with just a few good people. And better yet, because short schedules mean prompt deliverables, there is much less likelihood of a project delivering something that the users don't want. In a short project, there's not enough time between the definition of requirements and the delivery of the finished result for the business to change all that much.

Exercises — Making IT Personal

1. Look for QCSS Violations
Take a look at the process for defining your IT projects. Which of the four QCSS variables do you specify, and which ones are determined by the project estimate? Do you define Quality re-

quirements, or does Quality end up as the free variable that gets determined based on the specification of the other three?

2. Look for Non-Linearity in your Projects

Do you assume that doubling the resource will give you the finished product twice as fast? Find specific project examples where attempts have been made to add resource in order to accelerate schedule. What's your track record of success? What are you going to do differently to improve your track record for the future?

Chapter 10: How'd We Get into this Mess?

Why isn't Information Technology Simple?

There is a lot of complexity in Information Technology, but much of it is unnecessary. The complexity increases the magic of IT (see Chapter 1), and enhances the wizardry of the people in IT.

Secret 23: Information Technology seems more complex than it has to be.

At some level, everything in the universe is complex. Cooking is complex when we look at the actual chemical changes that food products go through in the process of becoming appetizing. Buildings are complex when we consider the ways that the structures interact with gravity and other forces of nature. The human body is extraordinarily complex in the way that all of the cells and cellular systems interact to keep us alive and healthy. But we live as humans every day, and we cook and we move through buildings without considering these things as complex. So why do we think of computer systems as more complex than these other processes?

No Simple Outer Layer

I think there are two reasons. First, each of these other examples of complexity has an outer layer — a simplistic view — that makes it appear simpler than it is. We learn about cooking without having to understand chemistry. We live in buildings without having to understand physics. And we live in our human bodies without having to know how our bodies work.

These processes appear to be simple and consistent. We cook something too long and it burns, no matter what the food is. Buildings sway in the wind and occasionally fall over in incredibly high winds or earthquakes. We cut ourselves accidentally, and we bleed. We understand the simple cause-and-effect relationships that insulate us from having to know the details of how cooking and architecture and physiology really work. We have a simple outer layer of logic that allows us to make decisions about these things without really understanding them.

It's the same thing with a car. Most of us have very little understanding of how a car works. We know about the accelerator pedal, the brake pedal, the steering wheel, and the gear shift, and that's about it. We know that we have to take the car in for maintenance once in a while. But because we deal with this simple model of a car, we don't have to understand gear ratios and gasoline/oxygen mixtures and how to provide more torque at lower speeds. We deal with a simple outer layer version of the car — not it's real mechanical nature.

But when it comes to information technology, we don't see an outer layer; we see only the confusion that comes from the details that poke out through the thin skin of the systems. We have to learn about firewalls and virus scanning, file formats and hundreds of other details that get in the way of the real purpose of the systems. If software doesn't work, reboot the computer, and it might work the second time, and we don't know why. Things are just too complicated, and, as a result, we treat information technology differently than other areas. We fear it. We despise it. We consider it an unfortunate necessary evil.

A lot of this problem comes from the immaturity of information technology. If we go back a hundred years or so, there was no simple outer layer to cars. Anyone who had a car had to be a mechanic just to keep it running. Breakdowns were constant, and it took mechanical skills to be able to drive. Those were the days when the trunk was for tools and the glove box was for the mechanic's gloves you wore when you made repairs.

Computers are under the hood today in a few areas, even literally under the hood in modern cars. But most information systems and personal computers are still unnecessarily complicated.

After fifty years or so of information technology, it's time for us to get out of the do-it-yourself mechanic mode. We ought to be able to treat most information systems the same way we treat car engines: use them for their basic purpose, keep the complicated stuff under the hood and away from the light of day, and occasionally have a mechanic look at the systems to make repairs.

Market Forces

If the absence of a simplified outer layer is the first reason for the apparent complexity of computer systems, what's the second reason? Surprisingly, computer systems appear overly complex because market and evolutionary forces make them that way.

Consider for a minute a different world in which cars never wear out. If you are a car maker, how will you compete in such a world? In this imaginary world there are only two reasons a consumer will replace a car: (a) the car is destroyed in an accident, or (b) the consumer sees benefit from a new car that offers more features. Assuming that car makers don't deliberately increase the number of accidents (I'll come back to this in a minute), their only choice for continued sales is to produce cars that have more features. This is the route that software makers have taken. They have a product that doesn't wear out (see Chapter 7 for the difference between hardware maintenance and software maintenance), and so they have to continually offer new software versions with new features in order to produce more revenue. What's the result of the new features? More complexity, more confusion, more of a training problem, and less likelihood that a simple outer layer can be used to understand their software products. So the durability of software is one of the primary contributors to software complexity!

Now let's go back to the other reason for replacing a car in a world in which cars don't wear out: the car is destroyed in an accident. I said that we could assume that car makers won't deliberately increase the number of accidents. But let's dig deeper into this idea. The accidents we're talking about are events in which the car is damaged to a point beyond repair. There's no obvious parallel in the software world, since software doesn't get into accidents. But is there a point at which software is damaged beyond repair? Surprisingly, yes. Although software continues to perform its original function indefinitely, there are two situations in which it can be damaged beyond repair. In the first situation, a defect ("bug") is discovered that becomes impossible to live with. And in the second situation, the environment around the software is changed so that the software no longer functions. For example, the software ran under the Windows 95 operating system, but won't work under the current version of the Windows operating system.

Normally, software makers issue periodic updates to their software, sometimes called maintenance releases, service packs, or upgrades. These updates fix defects and adapt the software to work in new environments like the current version of Windows. The software makers often charge consumers for these updates, but they usually differentiate between these updates and new versions of the same products. For new versions of the products, they charge a lot more, ostensibly under the assumption that the consumer is getting significant value for new features in the new software version.

To get even more revenue, software makers periodically discontinue support for older versions of their software products. This causes an artificial end-of-life for older product versions, since it means that eventually the owners of these older versions of software will have to replace the older versions with new software versions. So software makers don't increase the number of accidents, but they do something better: they make the older software versions obsolete, thus guaranteeing the eventual need for replacement.

Interestingly enough, though, it's usually not the software itself which forces obsolescence and replacement — it's the hardware: the computer on which the software runs. Unlike the software, the hardware will eventually wear out, and new replacement hardware will only work with the latest version of software. The car maker equivalent to this situation would be to have an alliance between car makers and gasoline producers in which the gasoline producers would periodically change the formula for gasoline, and the car makers would change the car design to use the new formula. Eventually your old car would become obsolete because you could no longer find the gasoline to run it, just as eventually old software becomes obsolete because you can no longer find the hardware to run it.

To summarize, market forces artificially require systems to be more complex in order to sell software. Software makers add features which may offer little benefit to most consumers, but which cause the software to get more and more complicated. Thus the "zero maintenance" advantage that software has over hardware is offset by a market that wants to sell you more software.

Evolutionary Forces

If this were the only reason for software complexity, then we would expect that off-the-shelf applications would be complex, but that computer systems developed internally within a company should be simple. We know they aren't simple, but why?

Consider the birth of a city. A city starts as a collection of buildings that gradually grows with the addition of more buildings, becoming a village and then a town, and then ultimately a city. Of course there's an initial reason for the growth; maybe there's a good natural port on a body of water, or a crossing of two major railroads or roads. Whatever the reason for the initial buildings and the ensuing growth, the city typically starts without much planning. People initially build whatever they want wherever they want, and roads are added based on convenience. As the community grows, a governing body emerges, and some rules are put into place. But initial rules usually focus more on the conduct of the citizens than on the need for construction control, and so it often isn't until much later that the governing body deals with issues of zoning, public utilities, and traffic management. By then a number of mistakes have been made, and so the city has to deal with construction that is "grandfathered" as exempt to the new rules.

Now compare this growth of a city to the growth of computer systems within a company. The computer systems usually start as individual systems that are purchased or developed by various people in the business for their own needs. There is little planning at this stage because most people view their systems as necessary only for their own individual purposes. Systems continue to grow and expand as the company grows and expands. If any of the systems are written by programmers specifically for the company (as opposed to off-the-shelf purchased software), then the programmers only address the specific needs of the person sponsoring the project — not the broader needs of the business.

A city without planning can be very confusing to a visitor. Residential and business areas aren't clearly defined; roads aren't well laid-out; and navigation through the city can be complicated.

Similarly, a business without systems planning can be confusing and complicated. Systems seem to overlap in their purposes; data is captured multiple times and entered in different databases; and it's difficult to get a single "right" answer to any business question.

There's a tendency to lump all of the computer systems in an enterprise together into a single view called the "information technology" of the company. And viewed as this lump, the information technology is often incredibly complex and confusing. But try to remember that most information technology in a company got there through a series of short-term decisions and purchases without any planning whatsoever. It was the lack of planning that created the complexity — not the systems themselves.

Dealing with IT Complexity

We've learned that IT is complex because of market and evolutionary forces, and that the absence of a simple outer layer makes IT seem even more complex than it is. But there are forces that make other systems more complex than they have to be, and we still manage to build a simple outer layer for them. Consider, for example, the way that car engines have become increasingly complex in the face of EPA regulations on emissions. Very little of that complexity has been passed on to the car buyer, because the complexity has been kept under the hood. So we have to accept responsibility for some of the IT complexity ourselves; we've created much of the complexity by the way we view our IT systems.

Let's go back to the city analogy. We can simplify our view of a city by describing it as a collection of areas. The areas might be neighborhoods, or shopping districts, or industrial parks, or recreational areas. The areas are linked together by primary roads or highways. Within an area there are secondary roads or streets which allow the people in an area to move between buildings.

We can also look at the city from the perspective of its utility services. We can view a map of sewer lines, water lines, power lines, telephone lines, gas lines, cable TV lines, etc. Each of these utility services has a network of stations and sub-stations which distribute the service across the city.

Now consider the information systems in a company. We can simplify our view of this information technology by describing it as a collection of functional areas that correspond to the primary functions performed by the business. There are systems which support sales, systems for operations or manufacturing, systems for accounting and payroll, etc. The systems are typically linked together by primary data flows, and within each system there are databases which store the data used by the individual system.

We can also look at the information technology from the perspective of its utility services. In this case we're talking about the computer servers, the local area network, Internet connectivity, maybe a wide area network, and the backup processes which accommodate the needs of the business during an emergency. Each of these utility services has stations and sub-stations just like the utilities of a city.

Information technology isn't as complex if it's described in a way that uses an outer layer that eliminates the need for unnecessary information. Even if the information technology in your company has grown without planning, there's still a simple way to view it. And it's important to find that simple way. If information technology is considered complex, then information technology decisions will be complex as well, and they will be very difficult to make. But if information technology is simplified to the point where it's easily understood by everyone in the company, then the decisions about information technology will be simple as well.

Don't be deceived by IT wizards who withhold key knowledge about your company information systems. Insist on a simple view of information and computer systems, relating proposed IT improvements to specific improvements in the business. Information technology decisions shouldn't be made for technology reasons — they should be made for business reasons.

Exercises — Making IT Personal

1. How does the IT organization in your company make IT more complex than it has to be? How do *you* make IT more complex than it has to be?

2. Think of some examples where evolutionary forces in your company have made IT overly complex. How can that complex view be changed?

3. Is there a simple "outer layer" that can be used to describe IT in your company? If not, then how will you create such an outer layer?

Note: See Chapter 8 for the description of an IT strategy process that you can use to help simplify your view of IT.

Chapter 11: Simple, Simpler, Simplest

How to Simplify Information Technology

In the previous chapter I explained why IT is considered to be complex. Here are some of the secrets of making it simpler.

Secret 24: The easiest way to simplify technology is to not use it at all.

One of the most obvious ways to keep things simple is to avoid using technology altogether. We get so used to having computer systems for every purpose that we sometimes forget the alternatives. Here's an example. I was managing the development of an Internet-based payroll system. The system would be used by small business customers who would enter their payroll updates over the Internet using a browser. We had some initial designs for the browser screens that would be used, and we wanted to get feedback from some customers.

Ask a technical person how to get this feedback, and there's a high probability that the technical person will suggest the use of a prototype system — software that acts like the real system. The problem with this approach is that it's often as difficult to put together the prototype as it is to develop the final software. And the customer feedback on the prototype is heavily influenced by factors that aren't relevant to the final system at all — things like the performance speed of the prototype, how errors are handled (typically not fleshed out in the prototype), and the way that mouse clicks work. What's more, when customers are presented with a computer prototype, they are more reluctant to make suggestions for big changes because they think the system has already been designed. They see the prototype not as a blank sheet of paper for their design feedback but instead as a system design that has been cast in concrete.

Instead of using a computer prototype, we did various screen designs in a word processor, and we printed them out for the customers to look at on paper. The customers were led through a paper-based exercise in which they considered how they would enter the data needed for a payroll.

The results of the paper prototype were fantastic. The customers gave us some really good tips for how to move fields from page to page to accommodate their needs. Suggestions were made to rearrange some of the flow from field to field, and some good comments were provided on other ways we could improve the usability of the system. We achieved superior results for a fraction of the cost of building a computer prototype. And because it was a paper-based prototype, we were able to quickly alter the screen designs, send the customers the new versions, and refine the design with multiple iterations. The result was a better system, and the customers who participated in the prototype evaluation were ecstatic because they saw their comments being applied.

There's a trap when we're dealing with computer systems; we tend to make things more complex than they have to be and use tools that may not be necessary. Think twice about whether there is a simpler way to do what you need to do; sometimes less technology is better.

Secret 25: Lack of focus leads to unnecessary complexity.
Follow the 80-20 Rule to focus on the important things, and
your IT will be simpler.

Vilfredo Pareto observed in the early 1900's that 80% of the wealth in Italy was held by 20% of the population. He went on to generalize this 80-20 rule to other areas. The idea became known as the Pareto Principle, and it continues to apply today. For example, approximately 80% of the beer consumed in the United States is sold to 20% of the people. Approximately 80% of the diapers consumed in the United States are bought by 20% of the families. And some studies claim that there is an overlap between the consumers of beer and diapers, so some supermarkets and convenience stores locate the beer and diapers close together in their stores.

But how does the 80-20 rule apply to systems design? The 80-20 rule would assert that 80% of the time spent in a system by a system user will be spent on 20% of the function. Thus it makes sense that the focus on improvements in system usability and performance should be made in this same 20% of the system. Clearly, an improvement in usability and system performance in a frequently used part of the system will provide more benefit to the business than an improvement in an area of the system that is seldom used.

How else can the 80-20 rule be applied? Maybe 80% of the benefit from a software upgrade will be derived from 20% of the features in the upgrade. So if you have any control over the features being included (this applies if the programmers doing the software are working for your company), then you ought to try to narrow down the feature set in order to maximize the return from the work being done.

There are uses for the 80-20 rule in almost every aspect of IT. For example, typically 80% of the support calls will come from 20% of the users; 80% of the hardware failures will come from 20% of the hardware components; and 80% of the software bugs will be found in 20% of the program code. The trick in seeing a use for the 80-20 rule is to pay attention to what's *not* happening. What users *aren't* making support calls? What hardware *isn't* failing? What software *isn't* revealing any bugs? If you keep thinking about things in this way, pretty soon you'll see a pattern. Then you can focus attention on the 20% that matters most, thus reducing effort and maximizing benefit.

Secret 26: Systems are unwieldy and complex because we let them get that way. To make systems simpler, keep project scope under control.

In Chapter 9 I described the four variables in a project: quality, cost, schedule and scope. Of these four, scope is the variable that most people have the hardest time understanding. Let me use a home building analogy to explain. Most people have a fairly good idea of what's behind the walls in a house, so it will come as no surprise that many house plans show kitchens and bathrooms clustered together in a house to share the plumbing (typically back-to-back or one on top of another if it's a multi-story house). If you're working with an architect to design a house, and you want to move one of these bathrooms to a different location in the house, then it's reasonable to expect that there will be a higher cost to run additional pipe to the new location.

If the construction on your house has already started, the plumbing has been done, and you *now* decide you want to move a bathroom to a different part of the house, then you'll expect an even higher cost. Pipe has to be redone, and the relocation of the bathtub may even require a structural change to the house.

If you wait even later in the house construction, and ask to move a bathroom after wallboard has been added to the walls, you'll find that the cost has gone up even higher. But you expect this, right? Because you have a basic knowledge of the home construction process, you understand that certain changes have to be made early, or there are consequences due to the impact of your change.

Now let's switch back to a discussion of Information Technology and the scope of an IT project. Just like in our home building example, there are decisions made in the design of an IT project that have consequences to the rest of the project. If decisions are made early on and then contradicted later, then there are architectural consequences to the change in scope. For example, if a system is designed for 5 simultaneous users and the scope is changed to support 500 simultaneous users, then this will typically have a very serious impact on the system. Major infrastructure components may be inadequate, and it's possible that the whole system will have to be redesigned.

What makes it more difficult in IT projects is that most business people don't have a good understanding of what's "behind the walls" in IT. Because of this lack of understanding, the business people don't have an intuitive grasp of the consequences of a scope change. Something that may seem trivial may in fact have a significant impact, while other changes that seem substantial might have very little impact at all.

This problem can be resolved with trust (see Chapter 2) and good communication. IT people who are good at defining projects and systems know which design issues are critical to resolve early and which issues can be resolved at a future date. The system requirements process is simplified because the designers focus on the critical issues at each stage of the process, and defer discussion of non-critical points until later. Just as you don't have to pick your carpet color when you determine your initial floor plan for a house, you don't have to make many of the system decisions up front. But the key to making the process successful is to work with an IT person who can differentiate between the various types of decisions, and to have a joint IT/user process that gets the major scope trade-offs out on the table for the decisions to be made.

Once the project is underway, there will inevitably be some scope changes. But to keep the project on track, it's important to try to offset every scope increase with a corresponding scope decrease in another area. This is the same process you would follow with a house when you're trying to keep the cost down, making trade-offs between various home features so that you can ensure a result that is both beneficial and economical.

Secret 27: Systems that are built in layers are much easier to manage and change.

Have you ever put together a home entertainment system? You can buy a complete system out of the box, but many people elect to assemble a home entertainment system from various components. They buy a television, a DVD player, a VCR or DVR, and a receiver to handle the audio. Then they buy speakers to actually produce the sound. Each of these components has a way of connecting to the other components, so all you have to do is to interconnect the components using the appropriate cables, and your home entertainment system is up and running.

The nice thing about the component approach is that you can upgrade various pieces of your home entertainment system whenever you like. If you decide that you need better speakers, just get the new ones and plug them in. If you want to upgrade your television to the newest wall-mounted plasma set, then just plug the new set into your other components.

The key to the success of a component-based home entertainment system is the use of standards for interconnection. Televisions connect to audio systems in a few standard ways, and most higher-end televisions support all of the different methods of connecting. Similarly, speakers are designed to be hooked up to just about any audio system, and DVD players are designed to be connected to televisions and receivers.

Using a standards-based method for interconnecting components seems like an obvious way to do things, and information systems can be designed using this same approach. Most modern information systems have at least three layers, and possibly more. At the bottom is the database layer, which manages the information in the database. Next is a process layer, which contains all of the business rules that are required for making decisions about your data. And at the top is the presentation layer, which allows users to interact with the process layer, and thus to interact with the data.

Many systems break the process layer into components, separating out the software for processes that are used in multiple systems, things like currency conversion and tax and shipping calculations. This ensures that these processes are always done consistently by every system, and it simplifies software maintenance when business processes change.

In some systems, there is another layer between the database layer and the process layer. This middleware layer (see Secret 11 in Chapter 4 for more on middleware) allows the process layer to get data from any appropriate database in your company.

And in a few systems, you'll find another batch process layer off to the side. The batch process layer is used for tasks which don't have to be performed immediately, but which can instead be performed later in the day as workload allows. Users can initiate a batch process in this layer, and then go on to do other things while the batch process is running.

Why would you design a system to have all of these layers? For the same reason that you'd build a home entertainment system using components: flexibility. For example, a system using this approach can be originally developed for a browser interface but can be easily adapted for a voice response interface later, so that your customers can get at your system over the phone. Or in another example, if you have specialized systems which get their data from your customer database and you change to a Customer Relationship Management (CRM) system, it will be relatively easy to adapt your old systems to access the new CRM database.

It's fairly common for older systems to have been designed more like the out-of-the-box home entertainment center: everything works but nothing is interchangeable. If you need to replace any part of this kind of system, then your IT organization will have to do some major work.

While it may be understandable how such a system was created in the first place, there's no excuse for developing new systems this way or for buying new systems which are built this way. Make sure your new systems are based on components with standard interfaces, in order to maximize your flexibility for the future.

Exercises — Making IT Personal

1. Can you think of any examples in your company where technology has been used for something that would have been easier with less technology?

2. How are you using the 80-20 rule (Pareto Principle) in your company? How are you using it in IT? If you aren't using it, where and when are you going to start?

3. Have you run into situations where changes in IT project scope have made a bigger difference in project size or duration than you would have thought? Did it come as a surprise or did your IT organization let you know up front that the scope change would make such a significant difference? How well do you communicate with your IT organization about requirements changes and their impact on overall project scope? What can you do to improve the communication?

4. What percentage of your company's systems are built in layers, with standardized interfaces between the layers? Are all of the newer systems built that way? If not, then why not? What steps, if any, are being taken to convert older systems to use layers?

Chapter 12: *Your* System was Bad Today

Building a Partnership

It's easy to love and praise a good child, but it's a little harder for a parent to accept responsibility when a child behaves badly. If you have children, then you've probably done this: When the child is good, then it's *your* child, but when the child is bad, then it's *your spouse's* child. "*Your* son was bad today at school," but "*my* son got an 'A' on his term paper."

In one sense, systems and data are just like children. If it's your idea to buy or build a system for your business, then you're like the proud parent for that system. You beam with pride when things go well and the system makes a significant difference in your company. And if there are problems, then sometimes you're committed to make things right, working hard to solve the problems and turn the system into a success. But there are other times when there's a tendency to treat a "bad" system just like a "bad" child: blame the problems on the other members of your family.

Secret 28: The Information Technology organization is your partner in creating and managing systems and data, with shared responsibilities.

That partnership can be like a marriage, with both marriage partners working together to make a better life. But like all marriages, there are times when problems cause disharmony between the marriage partners, and if you're not careful, that disharmony can lead to name-calling and blame.

Systems and processes are not solely the responsibility of their users, nor are they solely the responsibility of the Information Technology organization that creates and supports them. The responsibility is shared, and both partners have to continuously work to keep things moving in a positive direction.

How can we improve the working relationship between system users and their IT organization? It's important for each organization to establish ground rules on their roles and responsibilities. With a marriage you establish ground rules by talking about important things like "who will pay the bills?" as well as trivial things like "who will take out the trash?" With systems the discussion is more focused around issues like "who will be responsible for recognizing the need for a business change to the process?" (typically the system users), and "who will be responsible for making sure that the computers work the way they're supposed to? (typically the IT organization). With data, the discussion is focused around issues like "who will be responsible for entering valid data into the system?" (typically the system users), and "who will be responsible for managing the technical aspects of the data storage?" (typically the IT organization).

Just as there are no hard and fast rules for how responsibilities are assigned in a marriage, there are no rigid rules for how responsibilities should be assigned in a relationship with an IT organization. There are traditions, but there are sometimes exceptions. Ultimately, the "right" way to assign responsibilities is whatever works well for your business. The fact that responsibilities *are* assigned is more important than the particular *way* that the responsibilities are assigned. Most organizational relationship problems come from lack of definition of responsibilities or from disagreement on the way that responsibilities have been divided.

Here are some examples of the traditional assignment of responsibilities relating to Information Technology organizations:

System and Data Users	Information Technology Organization
"Use" the systems	Manage the computer hardware and software required by the systems
Enter valid data into the systems	Manage the physical storage of the data
Establish rules for validating data	Incorporate those rules into the software so that system users are prevented from entering data that doesn't conform to the rules
Define the overall business process	Recommend the use of technology to improve specific aspects of the business process
Clarify the specific parameters under which the system will run (e.g., number of users and their location, the transaction speed required, the level of audit trail required)	Let the users know which parameters are difficult or very expensive to satisfy. After discussion with users, implement a system solution that satisfies the important parameters while maximizing the benefit to the business

System and Data Users	Information Technology Organization
In using the system, discover any errors in the process or in the software, and report the errors to the IT organization	Investigate the cause of reported errors, and resolve the errors in the optimum way for the business
Recognize changing business needs, and recommend process, system and data improvements to meet those business needs	Recognize changing system requirements (e.g., due to increasing data volume), and recommend process, system and data improvements to meet those changing system requirements
Revise business processes and data entry to reflect changing business and system requirements	Revise software, hardware and database structure to reflect changing business and system requirements

Again, I want to point out that these role assignments are traditional, but that you can assign roles any way you want as long as things work. However, if you do choose to assign roles in a very non-traditional way, then you should recognize the difficulty of hiring people into the jobs required by those assignments. It is rare, for example, to find someone who is good at both using a system *and* writing the software for the system.

Stepsystems

The problem of parental responsibilities is compounded in a blended family. It can be difficult to deal with stepchildren who until recently haven't been your own. But it's much easier to accept stepchildren who behave well than to rise to the challenge and deal with stepchildren who are having difficulties.

"Stepsystems" are similar. A stepsystem is like a stepchild; you gain responsibility for it when you go into a new job or accept new responsibilities, just like gaining a stepchild when you marry someone who already has children. The system is already there; it might be working well or it might be full of problems. If it's working well, then you can relax and focus on making it even better. But if the system is full of problems, then you'll have to figure out what to do about them.

Secret 29: Emotionally, it's more difficult to deal with a system problem that you inherit in a new job.

You're not as committed to the system as the system creator was, and so there's a high probability that you'll want to make drastic changes or even discard the system altogether, perhaps replacing it with another system with which you're more familiar (but see Secret 7 in Chapter 3 and its explanation of the "I can't live without XYZ" phenomenon). You also have to deal with an existing assignment of responsibilities between your own department and the IT department. As with a second marriage, the responsibilities may not be allocated in a way that's familiar to you, and you may disagree with your predecessor's role.

Before you discard the current stepsystem and its assignment of responsibilities, think of how you would deal with a stepchild in a new marriage. Most people in that situation would proceed slowly and cautiously, getting to know the stepchild while reassuring the stepchild that this is a change for the better. Initial tolerance is needed while you assess the current situation. Only in the case of extreme stepchild behavior (e.g., drug use or criminal activity) should immediate action be taken. Otherwise it's best to develop a friendly relationship with the stepchild, assuring the child of your good intentions, and learning where compromise might be required on your part or on the part of the stepchild.

A similar approach should be taken with a new stepsystem. Fight your natural tendency to rebel against anything different from what you're used to. Talk to the system users and the IT organization to get an understanding of the positive and negative aspects of the system. Figure out how to build on what's been learned rather than to just tear it all down and start over. In the long run you'll accomplish more, and you'll be less distracted by secondary issues that don't directly contribute to business goals.

Exercises — Making IT Personal

1. Do you have a partnership between your system and data users and your IT organization? Or is it more of a rivalry or a feud? What steps can you take to develop a partnership?

2. Are the roles and responsibilities of your partnership with the IT organization explicitly defined? If not, then jointly work to define them.

3. How do the roles and responsibilities of your partnership with the IT organization differ from the traditional roles described in the examples in this chapter? Are there good reasons for any differences?

4. Think about a recent situation in which you, or someone your know, has inherited a stepsystem. How was the situation handled? How could it have been handled better?

Chapter 13: Parlez vous Anglais?

Dealing with IT People

There is a need for a wide variety of people in the world, and the mix of their various talents makes the combination of various people stronger than any one person would be individually. But with every strength comes a corresponding weakness, and the more specialized an individual person becomes in one area, the weaker that person becomes in other areas.

I'm going to make some comments about IT people in this chapter that may seem derogatory to some, but bear in mind that the particular skill set that makes someone good at working with Information Technology has its side effects. Most people who criticize the members of an IT organization couldn't do what they do on a day-to-day basis.

Secret 30: IT people are very focused on the how, not on the what. The most common mistakes they'll make are errors caused by doing the wrong things, not by doing things wrong.

Tell IT people what you want to do, and you can almost see the gears turning in their heads as they evaluate alternative approaches and eventually come up with various options on how to accomplish your goals. IT people are so focused on the *how*, in fact, that the most common mistakes they'll make are errors caused by doing the wrong things — not by doing things wrong. That's why an IT strategy (discussed in Chapter 8) is so important to a business; it's the only way to be sure that your IT organization is headed in the right direction.

In Chapter 2, I compared IT people to medical doctors, and in fact there are many similarities:

- Both doctors and IT people have in-depth knowledge of a technical speciality that goes beyond the knowledge held by everyone else. The science advances quickly, and both groups have to struggle to keep up with changing technology, techniques, and best practices. Continuing education and training are a must.
- Both groups of people are on call to handle problems 24 hours a day, seven days a week. Medical doctors deal with the lives of patients. IT people keep business systems running.
- Both medicine and IT use a different language that can intimidate outsiders. The mystical language contributes to the magic (see Chapter 1), and acts as a barrier to communications.

As I pointed out in Chapter 2, IT people aren't usually as savvy as doctors at communicating with non-technical people. Perhaps it's true in part because so many technical terms are in common use that the IT people can't determine the extent of your knowledge when they're talking to you. But this is no excuse, and it's important that IT organizations either train their people to communicate clearly or else hire spokespeople to act as translators.

Some of the worst difficulties in communicating with an IT organization are caused by differing definitions of non-technical words. For example, IT people frequently use the word "project" to mean the software development part of a larger "Project" that includes everything necessary for the business deliverable: design, building, testing, documentation, training, implementation, and infrastructure additions. Thus an IT organization completion date for a project may be viewed by IT as the completion of the software work. If you don't clarify the deliverable, then there will be a huge misunderstanding (thus leading to lack of trust).

Similarly, an IT organization might commit to have some work done by the third quarter. The IT customer will assume this means July 1, but the IT organization will assume it means September 30th at midnight.

Secret 31: The best way to communicate with an IT organization is to talk to members of the organization as if they're from a foreign country and don't speak English very well.

Explain things multiple times using different words each time, and have them repeat things back to you in their own words (this technique also works with medical doctors). The key to clear communication is to make no assumptions and leave no aspect of any commitment undocumented. You'll do yourself a favor, and you'll also be doing the IT organization a favor, since what they really want is the same thing you want: clear communication.

Secret 32: Motivate an IT organization the same way you'd motivate any other organization, by measuring its contribution to business success.

A lot of people believe that motivating an IT organization has to be done differently than motivating other parts of a business, but I disagree. The best way to get an IT organization to contribute to business success is to *measure* the organization's contribution to business success and then publicize the result. Reward members of the IT organization when they and the business are successful. And when things don't go well, look for process and motivation problems rather than scapegoats.

If left to their own devices, most IT organizations will suggest measurements of things that are more technical in nature — things like uptime (the percentage of time that a computer or system is available to its users), project completion percentage (the percentage of projects that are completed on time), and bugs fixed per month. The good thing about these types of measurements is that they can be easily calculated from existing data (which is why the IT people like them). But the bad thing about these measurements is that they don't necessarily correlate to business success or happy customers.

Take uptime as an example. If a particular system is used internally by your employees, and those employees use the system heavily on certain days of the month (e.g., month-end) and at certain times of the day, then what's really important to those employees is the availability of the system during those critical days and times. An average uptime over the whole month (especially if it includes nonworking hours) is pretty much meaningless to them. Moreover, what may be most important to those employees is the availability of a certain subset of the system — not the entire system that's being measured.

I've heard that at one point one of the phone companies attempted to measure its 411 directory assistance service solely by the number of calls completed per hour (and this is probably still one of the measurements that they track). But without taking customer satisfaction into account in the measurement, the directory assistance operators were motivated to fly through the calls without really providing much help to the 411 callers. The resulting customer complaints taught them to revise their measurement.

In Chapter 8, I described a process for defining an IT strategy for your business, and if you follow that recommendation, then you'll find it fairly easy to measure your IT organization. The IT strategy describes what's most important to the business and to the IT organization, and then ties specific plans directly to that list of critical items. If the IT strategy is defined correctly, then it's a road map to success. Measurement of performance against the road map should be all that is needed. IT employees who are given the road map know where they're going, and they understand whether they're on course or losing time on some side road. And in spite of the geekiness that's shared by many IT employees, they want more than anything to be of service to others. That's why a business measurement and motivational approach works for IT organizations: because IT employees want to contribute to company success just as much as anyone else.

Exercises — Making IT Personal

1. Does the IT organization in your company seem to focus on the *how*? Has that led to problems where the IT organization does something well, but it's the wrong thing?

2. Does your company have an IT strategy (see Chapter 8) to keep the IT organization focused on doing the best things for your company?

3. What measurements do you use for your IT organization? Are they technical measurements like the ones I mentioned in the chapter, or are they measurements that really relate to business success? Do you even know whether your IT organization contributes to business success?

4. If you're not measuring your IT organization based on business success, then what are you going to do to change this?

Chapter 14: Sprechen sie Business?

Dealing with Business People

The IT industry term for business people is "users" because the business people make *use* of technology. But it's appropriate that the same word is applied to people who are addicted to drugs; in both cases the users have a dependency on something outside their control, it costs a lot of money, and they have to rely on a supplier organization to fulfill their needs. Just like drug dealers, many of the people in the IT organization have a love/hate relationship with their users; the IT people depend on the users for employment, but they may not sympathize with what the users are trying to do. This is especially true for people at lower levels in an IT organization who are often more focused on the fun of solving problems than on a detailed understanding of a user requirement or how the fulfillment of that requirement will improve things in the business. Sometimes this focus is merely a way of coping with frustration, since many IT projects are more political than practical or more cosmetic than critical.

In Chapter 13 I looked at IT people from the business point of view. Now I'll turn things around and look at business people from the IT point of view. Based on Secret 30 in the last chapter ("... The most common mistakes [that IT people will] make are errors caused by doing the wrong thing, not by doing things wrong.") , you might think that business people would be the exact opposite, but that's not true. Just like IT people, business people are more likely to make mistakes by doing the wrong thing. And it's even more specific than that.

Secret 33: Although business people want long-term success, they easily get caught up in the apparent urgency of shorter-term goals. The most common mistakes they'll make are errors caused by a focus on inappropriate shorter-term goals.

This focus on shorter-term goals is very common; maybe it's because people are overwhelmed by the sheer size and generality of the long-term objectives that executives define (e.g., "grow the business by 20%," "increase profitability by 5%"). Whatever the reason, the result is that business people look at each of these longer-term objectives, quickly translate the longer-term objectives into a series of shorter-term goals, and then doggedly pursue the shorter-term goals while forgetting the longer-term objectives that generated the shorter-term goals in the first place.

It's like a football player returning a kickoff from his own 20 yard line. He sees the goal line in the distance but his focus is on all of the opposing team's players standing in the way. Overcoming the short-term obstacles is a more immediate concern because he knows that the goal line can't be attained unless he defeats or avoids all of those obstacles.

The big difference, however, between the football player and the business person is that the goal line doesn't change for a football player while the play is in progress. That's not true for many business objectives, which change due to evolving business conditions relating to the customer, the market, the competition, the economy and new technology. So although it's reasonable for the football player to focus on short-term goals during a play, it's important for the business person to periodically reevaluate the approach being used to achieve the longer-term objectives, in order to make sure that the short-term goals shouldn't be changed.

Even if the short-term goals don't change, the business-to-IT relationship is endangered by the tendency of business people to keep the longer-term objectives to themselves, along with many of the short-term goals, and not to share this information with the IT people. Let me illustrate the problem with an example.

Suppose that you have an room in your home that you would like to improve. Ultimately you want to expand it, change the wall color, make it more light and airy, and install a bunch of high-tech audio-visual gear. You break this down into short-term goals and you go to a contractor to get help.

The first goal you give the contractor is to "make the room more light and airy." Accordingly, the contractor knocks out the exterior walls of the room and replaces those walls with floor-to-ceiling glass windows.

Next, you tell the contractor that you want to change the wall color, so the contractor patches and sands the wallboard and then gives the interior walls two coats of paint.

For your next goal, you tell the contractor that you want to install a big wall-mounted plasma TV, built-in speakers, and an in-wall cabinet for electronic equipment. The contractor cuts big holes in the interior wall, installs lots of cable, adds your built-ins as you requested, and then repaints the wall to cover up the damage.

Finally you go to the contractor and say that the room has to be bigger: at least 10 feet longer and 10 feet wider. Frustrated by your lack of foresight, the contractor tears out most of the work done previously and expands the room to your specifications.

You see the problem? Keeping the longer-term objective to yourself has cost you money and time because of rework and changes. The definition of short-term goals based on long-term objectives wasn't done in conjunction with the contractor, and so the short-term goals weren't sequenced in a way that optimized the overall process.

Now you probably think this example is pretty absurd, but I remember a photo in a Baltimore newspaper about twenty years ago. The photo showed a road crew repaving part of a street after digging it up to work on some part of the Baltimore infrastructure – I think it was storm drains. But the photo also showed another road crew coming down the street about a block behind the first crew, and this second crew was systematically digging up the freshly repaved road in order to work on a different part of the Baltimore infrastructure. The situation was funny and yet sad; obviously the two Baltimore departments had not communicated with each other, and their focus on short-term goals had blinded them to the longer-term objective of economical maintenance of the city's infrastructure.

That's what happens with business people as well. If the senior business executives are doing their jobs then all of the business people start on the same page with the same overall high-level business objectives. But as action plans to achieve those high-level business objectives are put together, and as long-term objectives and then short-term goals are defined, it's easy for the short-term goals to get out of alignment with the high-level business objectives. By the time a typical IT organization is brought into the picture, the linkage between the short-term goals and the high-level business objectives is long gone. A good IT systems analyst will attempt to get an understanding of the true objectives so that a system can be optimized for current and future business needs. But in many cases the true objectives are concealed behind the short-term goals that are being used to justify the project, and it's not possible for the IT person to rebuild the linkage to long-term objectives. The result is often a situation like the example with our contractor: high rework and correspondingly high expense, plus an unhealthy amount of frustration for the people doing the rework

Secret 34: Like IT people, some business people are also some-what focused on the how, but often inappropriately so. Overly-specific definition of system requirements by the business is a leading cause of excessive IT spending and low IT morale.

Business people have a habit of asking for their systems to work *exactly* a certain way, even if the cost of doing the project that way exceeds any benefit the business will derive (this is similar to the "I can't live without XYZ" phenomenon described in Chapter 3). As a result, it's easy for IT people to get disillusioned as they face the practical reality that they are rewarded for making specific users happy – not for improving things in the business.

Here's an example. A typical project starts with a statement of requirements from a business user. The best requirements are worded in terms of an overall business objective (e.g., "cut administrative time associated with a new order by half"), but unfortunately most business users already think they have a solution to their process problem, and so the requirement is usually stated in more specific – but more misleading – terms (e.g., "change the order entry screen to put all of the fields on one page instead of two pages). IT people vary in their reaction to such a specific request. Some "push back" at the requirement, trying to get an understanding of what the user is really trying to accomplish. Often this results in a more in-depth analysis of the real problem and so it leads to a better solution. But just as often, there is negative reaction to the push back; some business users don't want to be second-guessed, they think they know what they want, and IT people are not always good enough in their communication skills to be diplomatic with their push-back technique. Many business people get annoyed when IT people try to do analysis work for them, and they even get angry.

Experienced IT people have lived through situations like this hundreds of times, and have seen both good and bad results from pushing back. Depending on the particular user, the IT person may elect to "just do what he's told," whether or not it makes any sense for the business. The biggest danger from this concession is that the true nature of the problem may come to light during the work on the project, delaying the project or even leading to its cancellation. And if the project does reach its planned conclusion, then any failure of the project to achieve business benefit will likely be blamed on IT rather than on the project initiator. The bigger the project, the more likely it is that IT will be blamed. It's a "damned if you do and damned if you don't" situation for IT, but it happens every day.

Let's go back to those Standish Group statistics on project failure described in Chapter 6 and think about them from the IT perspective. Many of those late and over-budget IT projects were crippled by project scope changes during the course of the project. And many of the abandoned projects were caused by erroneous project requirements and invalid assumptions. Sure, IT people make mistakes now and again – we all do – but the cause of most IT project failures isn't in IT; it's in the communication between business and IT.

Compounding the problem from the IT perspective is the recent trend of sending IT work outside the company and in many cases outside the country (see Chapter 15 for more on outsourcing and offshoring). IT work is less expensive in other countries, but the already huge people communication problems are made worse by distance and by language differences. Sure, offshore resources do IT projects cheaper; they may even do the projects quicker. But expense and speed are irrelevant if the wrong work is being done in the first place, which is often the case if the business requirements aren't correct, or if the requirements come from personal preferences instead of business objectives.

Offshore work kills IT morale as well. IT people see most of the fun jobs going overseas, and many of the jobs left behind are just administrative roles for people who need to coordinate the offshore work. The decline in IT morale has filtered down to colleges and universities, and enrollment in IT degrees is in sharp decline.

Secret 35: Good IT analysis work can ensure that the real problem is being solved – not just a symptom. But a business focus on symptoms will prevent work on the real problems.

In Chapters 2 and 13, I compared IT people to medical doctors, so I'll continue that analogy by looking at things from a doctor's viewpoint.

Doctors know that patients are often wrong when they diagnose themselves. That's why doctors take the patient's self-diagnosis as just one piece of evidence in a list of things to consider. For non-obvious maladies, doctors will look at a detailed history of the patient along with various laboratory tests. Sometimes it turns out that the patient's diagnosis (e.g., a sore arm) is just a symptom of a broader problem (e.g., a bad heart).

The same thing happens in IT; a business person often observes and reports a problem that's really just a symptom of a different and potentially bigger problem. For example, a stockroom manager may report that inventory numbers in the computer system don't correspond to the true quantity of items on hand. The underlying cause of the discrepancy could be a whole range of things: a software error, a bad bar code scanner, an inconsistently used and unenforced process for scanning items when they're removed from inventory, theft, or even a combination of these factors. A good IT person will try to gather enough information to get to the bottom of the real problem, just as you would expect a doctor to gather evidence before making a diagnosis.

We sometimes get frustrated with a doctor when the process seems so involved – "it's just a sore arm; what's the big deal" – but doctors will persist in their thoroughness because they know that what they're doing is in the patient's best interest. This persistence is drilled into the doctors in medical school and during their internship, and doctors know not to be intimidated by a pushy patient who wants faster results.

This same persistence is, unfortunately, not common in IT people. Most IT people have received little training in problem diagnosis, and only a handful have received any advice on how to deal with a pushy business person. As a result, you'll find very few IT people who will stand their ground when confronted with an angry system user who wants an immediate solution to an apparent problem. A few will follow the approach of a doctor: first alleviate any life-threatening symptoms, then figure out what the real problem is. But many IT people will stop working on the problem after the initial symptom has been diminished.

Compounding this issue is the fact that many business people will refuse to approve funds for a solution to the real problem. As soon as a symptom such as a system outage is alleviated, they'll go back to their own work and let the real problem (e.g., insufficient server capacity) drop to the bottom of their priority list. This sometimes happens with medical patients as well, but most patients have enough common sense to actually do something about a medical problem and not just wait for the next occurrence of the inevitable symptom.

Secret 36: Telling someone in the IT organization about a problem doesn't mean that the IT organization is committed to fix it; but business people tend to see things that way.

Business people who have acquaintances in the IT organization are fond of visiting the IT people and telling them about problems that need to be solved. Most IT people love a challenge and they love to please, so quite often the IT people will begin work on helping the business person with the problem even though the work assignment didn't go through normal channels.

Of course this practice of "doing an end run" around IT departmental management isn't just something that business people do with the IT organization; it's a popular approach for getting things done throughout the business. But it's a particular problem in dealing with IT because of the susceptibility of the IT people to the temptations of pleasing a business user.

Ultimately this vulnerability in the IT organization ends up making things worse for everyone. Almost every IT organization has more work requested that it can do, and most good IT organizations have a prioritization process which attempts to ensure that IT effort provides maximum payback to the business (see Chapters 5 and 8 for more on how to choose the right projects). When this process is bypassed, the high priority work gets pushed aside based on low-level business demands, and the most important projects end up running late and over budget.

In good IT organizations, specific rules are in place about getting new work approved. Often there are designated people within the IT organization who can commit to take on new work, and it is made clear to the business – and the IT people – that requests made to anyone else will be rejected. If this seems harsh then consider a similar situation with a contractor working on remodeling your home – a contractor who's working to an aggressive schedule and fixed budget. Would you want someone in your family to be able to talk to a laborer and change the specifications for a room without going through the contractor? How about someone in your family who wants to do something more major like relocating a bathroom in the floor plan? Are you prepared to deal with the expense and schedule slippage that would result? Probably not, and the same can be said for IT.

Unfortunately, despite rules that may be in place, most business people tend to make suggestions to IT people as part of their normal day-to-day conversations. That's OK, but the IT people should be very conscious of their words in response to those suggestions. IT people should avoid the appearance of a commitment when none is intended, both to suggestions for unapproved work as well as suggestions for unapproved changes to existing projects.

Secret 37: The best way for IT to communicate with a business user is by using the language of the business – not the language of IT.

I was once a speaker in front of a group of CIO's, discussing some of the issues facing IT organizations. One of the CIO's asked me what he could do to better communicate his problems to his business users who seemed to have trouble understanding the difficulties associated with making changes to software. I suggested that he rephrase the problems in the users' terms instead of using the traditional IT terminology. This is fairly common advice, but I'm always amazed at how few people actually use this approach. IT people keep falling back on the language they use with their peers, instead of trying to understand the business user's point of view, and explaining things in user terms.

Here are two interesting examples of explaining IT in user terms. At Southern Company, CIO Becky Blalock had a breakthrough in communication when she explained IT in terms that are more understandable at a power generation company. She told her business users that just as Southern Company uses coal to generate power and then distribute the power to its customers, the Southern Company IT organization uses data to generate information and then distribute it to the business users. The business users got the point, and they began to understand some of the similarities between power distribution and the distribution of information.

At The Home Depot, Chief IT Architect Barbara Sanders used a similar approach to define the stages that new technologies go through before they were implemented in a live production environment. Her architecture organization issued "building permits" to pilot projects for new technologies, and then delivered a "certificate of occupancy" when the pilot was proven and the technology was ready for general release. Everyone at Home Depot understood exactly what that meant, and there were far fewer questions about why a new technology wasn't yet in use.

I've used similar approaches myself. At an architectural firm that specialized in designing college campuses and the buildings that go with them, I explained a plan for a future intranet by showing a campus metaphor for the intranet. Users enter the intranet through the "quad" in the middle of the campus, and then enter various "buildings" (subsystems), always coming back to the quad to navigate from building to building. I identified virtual classrooms for training, a "history department" that keeps records of the buildings the firm has designed in the past, a virtual library of white papers and presentations, an engineering library of details for Computer Aided Design (CAD), and even a transit station for "public transportation" to take the intranet user to selected areas of the Internet. By translating difficult technical concepts like home pages, databases, and gateways into terms with which the architects were familiar, I was able to help the firm understand the benefits of an intranet, as well as some of the issues they would encounter during construction.

For a lower level of explanation, I've often tried to relate IT issues to things that are familiar to the average person. For example, I've frequently used a plumbing analogy like the one in Chapter 11 to help explain why a system change is so difficult. I describe a hypothetical house-building project, and ask why it might be a big problem if the homeowner changes the location of a bathroom after the wallboard is up. The answer is obvious to most people, yet the concept of a difficult system maintenance change (like expanding a purchase order number) is in no way intuitive to these same individuals. Using the plumbing analogy makes the issues clear.

Similarly, most people seem to be able to relate to an example of trying to add four additional floors to a house that has a foundation designed for a single floor; they know that such a change will necessitate some major foundation work. But it's usually extremely difficult to directly explain why, for example, a system designed in Microsoft Access for a single user can't be easily expanded to be available for hundreds of users on an intranet.

For additional perspective, think of the problems that doctors have in telling their patients about complex diseases and their treatment. The best doctors are able to get their message across using examples from cars, plumbing, electrical circuits, construction, and other generally understood processes. Other doctors just throw medical jargon at you and expect you to figure it out. Which kind of doctor inspires more trust? Which kind of doctor would you rather have do your surgery? Amazingly, we base our opinion of a surgeon's competence not on his or her surgical abilities, but on the ability to communicate with the patient.

IT is the same kind of thing. Since business users can't judge the IT organization's technical ability, they base their judgment of IT on the ability to communicate clearly. Communication is an important part of every project, but it's especially important when business users don't understand what their IT organizations do for them. The next time IT people have to explain something, try having them use an analogy that business users can better understand. You'll find that communication improves, and the IT organization will get a lot more support.

Exercises – Making IT Personal

1. Are there situations in your business where short-term goals are being pursued even though they don't seem to support any longer-term business objectives? Are there shorter-term goals which conflict with current longer-term business objectives even though the shorter-term goals may have once been beneficial? What should be done?

2. When business requirements are given to the IT organization, how often are the business requirements put into context by telling the IT organization the short-term goals and longer-term objec-

tives that justify the requirements? The more you do this, the better the IT organization will be able to help the business.

3. Are business requirements that are given to IT ever "too specific" (see secret 34) so that the real objective of the requirements is obscured by the detail? What can be done to change this?

4. Are there situations where IT is constantly dealing with symptoms instead of solving the real problems? If so, then what can be done to ensure that the problems are solved?

5. Is there a clear, well-defined process in your business for getting IT projects approved? How about for getting IT project changes made? How often is this process subverted by informal communication between business people and IT people? What are the consequences? How will you change things to solve the problem?

6. What language does your IT organization use when communicating with the business people: the language of IT or the language of the business? What can you do to improve the situation?

Chapter 15: Have Your "Guy" Do It

Should IT be Outsourced? Offshored?

When we talk about dealing with IT people, it's natural for the subject of outsourcing to come up. Some of the IT professions, particularly those having to do with software development, testing and support, can be readily performed by people outside your company (outsourcing) or even outside your country (offshoring). In this chapter I'll talk about the pros and cons of having some of your IT work done outside your company.

Secret 38: Parts of IT can be outsourced or offshored, but it's a business decision, with risks and rewards.

Let's look at outsourcing. If it doesn't make sense to outsource an IT capability that's currently being performed by company employees, then it certainly doesn't make sense to offshore that capability. Offshoring is really just a special form of outsourcing.

Based on my experience, a company should consider outsourcing when one of the following criteria is met:

1. The vendor can do the job better than your company, at a reasonable cost.

2. The vendor can do the job just as well as your company, but the vendor is less expensive.
3. The vendor can't do the job as well as your company, but the vendor is less expensive, and the vendor does a "good enough" job.
4. The vendor may not do the job as well as your company, but the need for the job is uneven, cyclical, or unpredictable. As a result, it would be easier and less expensive to have a vendor do the job than to maintain a workforce in your business to deal with the uneven demand.

When Shouldn't You Outsource?

Here are some outsourcing disadvantages:
1. You increase risk because you create a dependency on a single point of failure over which you have very little control. Risk is even higher if the vendor is dealing with your customers (like outsourced customer support), or if the vendor is handling an aspect of your business that differentiates your company from its competition.
2. The process becomes more rigid, and is more difficult to change. An outsourcing business can only be profitable if the vendor has set up extremely well-defined processes. You may have to conform to the vendor's processes, follow the vendor's rules, and give up the flexibility that you had with your own resource.
3. You have to invest in a one-time expense to negotiate the out-sourcing contract, work out all of the processes that you will use in relating to the vendor, determine the details of how the vendor will be measured and compensated, and handle the transition to the vendor's services. In a large outsourcing deal, this is a huge undertaking.

Most outsourcing starts out as a financial decision, but it's important that you go beyond finance to evaluate risk and return.

Outsourcing your cleaning service may have very low risk, but outsourcing the development of a key company product is a whole different story. It's important to put together a risk mitigation plan as part of the early investigation into outsourcing, including the answers to questions like:

1. What are the risks? Specifically what could go wrong?
2. What are the consequences if each of those things happens?
3. What could you do to minimize the probability of those things happening?
4. What would you do if they happen anyway?
5. If things don't work out with this vendor, what options do you have? How difficult would it be to move the job to another vendor? To bring the job back in-house?

If the risks are too high, or you're not prepared to handle the consequences of things going wrong, then you shouldn't be looking at outsourcing.

Why Offshore?

I'll define offshoring as outsourcing work to a vendor outside your own country. I can think of only three reasons why you might want to outsource your work to an "offshore" vendor:

1. It's less expensive. This is the primary reason for offshoring in the IT world. Outsourcing to a country with a low cost of living or with a favorable exchange rate can be considerably less expensive than outsourcing to someone local.
2. The vendor may offer better quality. I don't hear this reason so much any more, although it was common in the electronics industry at one time. Some offshore software vendors claim to have better quality, but I haven't seen any statistics about actual work done by these vendors.
3. You can take advantage of time zone differences. For example, to provide customer support in off hours, or to have program-

mers implement your designs during the night to be ready the next morning.

Note that these three reasons don't replace the initial four outsourcing criteria — they just add another dimension to the decision. First you should look at whether you want to outsource, then you should look at whether you want to outsource to an offshore vendor. If it's too risky to outsource in the first place, then an offshore vendor won't change the situation. If an outside vendor can't do a job as well as your own people, then you either say "no" to outsourcing or you figure out whether the vendor can do a "good enough" job.

What's "good enough"? That depends on the situation. Dell recently changed one of its offshore vendors because customers complained about service from offshore workers. In Dell's case, it wasn't good enough.

Additional Disadvantages of Offshoring

All of the disadvantages of outsourcing apply to offshoring, but offshoring introduces a few more things to watch out for:

1. Language barriers can cripple an offshoring relationship. If you thought it was tough for a business user to work out the details of a process with an IT person, wait until they try to do it with an IT person who speaks English as a second language. Be sure that any offshoring agreement makes it clear who will be talking to whom, and that language proficiency requirements are spelled out.

2. Currency fluctuation can change your costs unless you make sure your pricing is defined in your own country's currency. And even if your price is protected, that just shifts the currency fluctuation risk to the vendor, who has to absorb the cost. If your vendor becomes unprofitable, then the vendor may try to change the contract, or even go out of business.

3. Your agreement is at the mercy of international politics. Things we take for granted, like safe locations for work, are not as guaranteed in certain countries. Trade embargoes and wars between nations could impact your offshore vendor, or even cut off your access to the vendor. One offshore vendor I worked with had a "disaster recovery plan" that called for all of the workers to get in their cars and drive to a neighboring country when their government collapsed. Problems like this make power outages appear trivial in comparison.

4. Legal agreements may be difficult to enforce. You can go after the local representative, but they probably don't keep very much capital in your country. So be very careful to avoid paying in advance for work unless money is held in a trustworthy in-country escrow account.

5. Crimes may be difficult to prevent, investigate and prosecute. If someone in another country steals your intellectual property, or uses your customer data for identify theft or credit card fraud, then you'll have a hard time pursuing the thieves. Criminal investigation and enforcement varies from country to country, and it may be difficult to bring the criminals to justice, must less obtain reimbursement or compensation for the victims of the theft.

So What Should You Do?

Think of offshoring as an extreme form of outsourcing. All of the same outsourcing rules apply, and there are a lot more risks. But the much lower cost of offshoring has fundamentally altered the mathematics of the outsourcing decision, tipping the balance of the equation away from keeping work in-house. That's why offshoring is in the news; it's very attractive to consider cutting some of your costs by 50 – 90%, even if it means eliminating local jobs.

When considering outsourcing however, make sure that you take steps slowly, starting with the easiest, most well-defined part of a process to outsource and working your way up the scale of process complexity. There are parts of IT (or any other organization) that you'll never want to outsource, but where you draw the line will vary from company to company. Most companies keep people in-house to do strategy, project management, requirements definition, and any function that is highly critical or highly confidential, or that provides significant competitive differentiation.

Exercises — Making IT Personal

1. Make two lists of the processes in your company that might qualify for outsourcing. For the first list, look at entire organizational functions like payroll, accounting, human resources, marketing, sales, manufacturing, etc., and major subsets of each of these functions. For the second list, look at skill sets and resources like building maintenance, shipping and receiving, infrastructure support, secretarial resources, software development and maintenance, etc. Apply the criteria described in this chapter to both lists, and identify likely candidates for outsourcing or offshoring.

2. Look at your competition. What are they outsourcing or offshoring? How is that working for them.

3. Identify companies who aren't direct competitors to your company, but who are outsourcing a capability that you'd like to consider outsourcing as well. Talk to people in these companies to get ideas of what to do and what not to do. Learn from their mistakes.

Chapter 16: Who's the Designated Driver?

How to Improve Your IT Organization

I mentioned in Chapter 10 that drivers of early cars had to be car mechanics as well, due to the unreliable nature of the vehicles they drove. As the vehicle technology matured, that requirement because less and less necessary, and the two tasks of driver and car mechanic separated.

The same thing is happening to Information Technology. The "driver" part of using IT is separating from the "mechanic" part of IT, just as it has for cars and for other technologies in the past. The mechanic part of IT is fairly well understood; it's the care and feeding of the technology infrastructure and the upgrading of that technology infrastructure as required by the business (the parts of IT that I've labeled as Infrastructure and Maintenance in this book). But what is the "driver" part of IT?

Let's go back to a clarification of what driving a car is all about. Driving is navigating a car from one place to another, avoiding obstacles, choosing optimum routes, and making most appropriate use of the tool (the car) you have available. In most cases, it's not cutting new roads; it's following existing roads, but picking the best combination of roads to avoid traffic and get to the destination in the most expedient way.

Take those words and apply them to Information Technology, and you get the following:

Driving IT is navigating a business from one place (level of business processes) to another, choosing optimum routes, and making most appropriate use of the technology you have available. In most cases, it's not inventing new ways of doing things; it's just applying other people's techniques to your own business, picking the best approaches to avoid disruption and get to a higher level of efficiency and effectiveness in the most expedient way.

Secret 39: When you look past the technology itself, IT is all about change: changing the business in ways that make it more efficient and effective.

If you don't need change, then you don't need IT — you just need infrastructure management. But change is a part of life, particularly in a capitalist economy in which your competitors are constantly changing to be better than you.

So if Information Technology can be thought of as having two components — the mechanic component to keep systems working (made up of Infrastructure and Maintenance), and the driver component to take a business to a higher level through the use of information technology — then I think we can all agree that most IT organizations have the mechanic component covered. That is, the IT organization performs the basic functions necessary to keep infrastructure working and to keep systems up-to-date. I'm not saying that they necessarily do it well, but at least they clearly have responsibility for it.

The responsibility for the other component — the driver component — is sometimes vested in the IT organization, but not always. Some IT organizations don't drive at all, but just take orders from other parts of the company, or from an executive to whom the IT organization reports. Some companies have other non-IT organizations to define technology direction, to prioritize projects and to define system requirements. These other organizations might be called Process Management or Quality Improvement or Process Improvement or Change Management, or the function might even be part of Marketing or Finance.

If you've got the driver component embedded in a non-IT organization and it's working for you, then that's great. I don't think it matters *where* the function is as long as it exists somewhere and the function is being carried out.

But I've seen a lot of companies who assume that the driver component is being done in the IT organization, and yet the IT organization doesn't have the resources or the skill set to support the need. If that's your situation, then your company is in trouble. You're like a ship without a compass or a construction crew without an architect. You can get things done, but it's anybody's guess whether you're headed in the right direction or whether you're doing anything productive that will stand the test of time.

Most IT organizations do not employ people who are change agents. Instead, the IT organizations usually start as infrastructure support groups, and they expand their capabilities from there. Because of this orientation toward the care and feeding of technology, the IT organizations tend to be built around the technology, rather than around the needs of the business and its customers. IT employees are hired for their technology skills — not their people and business skills. As the technology gets more and more complex, the wall between IT and everyone else gets higher. Projects get thrown over the wall from the user side, and systems get thrown back over the wall from the IT side. The groups operate like two underground tectonic plates pushing against each other, and the pressure builds until one day an earthquake occurs, and someone wakes up and says "IT is failing."

It doesn't have to be this way, but you can't count on an IT organization to fix itself. There are two sides to a wall, and if you allow the wall to be built between yourself and IT then you're just as much at fault as they are. If you have an existing wall, then remember that the wall can be torn down from either side.

If you don't feel that the IT organization in your company is doing all that it can do, here's what you can do about it. First, make sure you're not alone in these feelings. Check with peers and others higher-up in the organizational chart. Find out whether the feelings are shared.

Second, decide whether there is an efficiency problem, an effectiveness problem, or both. Efficiency is doing things well, while effectiveness is doing the right things. If you think your IT organization is doing the right things, but not very well, then you have an efficiency problem. If you think your IT organization isn't doing the right things, then you have an effectiveness problem. If you have both problems, then focus on solving the effectiveness problem first.

Improving Effectiveness

Most effectiveness problems are due to a difference of opinion over what should be done. The difference of opinion may be due to confusion over roles, or it may be a conscious disagreement on what the roles should be (see Chapter 12). It's also possible that there isn't adequate resource available to do the roles the way they ought to be done, and that the IT organization has redefined its role downward to fit limited resource and budget.

Secret 40: To increase the effectiveness of an IT organization, align direction, leadership and resources.

At a simplistic level, this means that direction has to be clear, that IT leadership is taking the IT organization in the specified direction, and that there are enough resources available to make progress toward the specified direction.

The reality is more difficult. Let's start with direction. It's easy to say that direction for Information Technology should come from the business, but who, specifically, should provide that direction? In most larger companies there is no single person who sets the direction for the company itself, much less for technology use by the company. In Chapter 2, I compared IT people to medical doctors but noted that the goals of a medical procedure are much more clear-cut than the goals of IT. In Chapter 3, I described the "I can't live without XYZ" phenomenon, which leads IT on various wild goose chases as the IT organization tries to answer specific demands from business people who over-specify their needs. In Chapter 5, I described the problems inherent in the project selection process that is used by most companies, and I pointed out that the measurement of strategic alignment is often missing from the project selection process altogether.

Chapter 8 describes a good way to create an IT strategy for a company. Its initial steps are better performed with participation from business executives, but I recognize that getting that participation may be difficult. If you're leading an IT organization and you want to put together an IT strategy following the steps in Chapter 8, then I encourage you to take your own best shot at understanding and defining the business objectives of your company. I've found that even if you can't get participation from business executives to create a set of business objectives, you can usually get feedback from them on a set of draft business objectives that you prepare yourself. Most business executives devote more time to reviewing and evaluating the work of others than they do to creating things themselves, so use the criticism to help you refine your IT strategy.

Once you have an IT strategy, you have a direction, so let's move on to the second element required to increase IT effectiveness: leadership. There has to be a single person who acts as the focal point for leading IT. The person doesn't have to be in the IT organization, and IT leadership doesn't even necessarily have to be the person's full-time job. But IT leadership has to be an important aspect of the person's job, and the leader has to be committed to the task.

The IT leader has two responsibilities. First, the IT leader has to paint a clear picture of future IT direction so that everyone in the company can understand and visualize where IT is going, everyone will appreciate that the future direction is better than where things are now, and everyone in the company will want to go there. Thus, the IT leader has to be a skilled communicator and motivator.

The second responsibility of the IT leader is to focus the company on the steps that have to be taken to achieve the desired IT direction. There are two important aspects of focus: concentrating effort where it's needed, and preventing work on things which aren't relevant or productive. The second aspect of focus is often forgotten, but it's critical for IT effectiveness. Unfortunately, most people will support work on things which are clearly important, as long as you work on their own (potentially unimportant) projects as well. Being an IT leader means persuading sponsors of non-critical projects that their work shouldn't be done.

Once you have direction and leadership, you need the third element: resources. This includes people as well as technology resources like computers, software and networks. It includes resources inside your company as well as resources you may engage on a contract or temporary basis. The ultimate measure of resources is money; the more money you have available, the more resources you can bring to bear on achieving your desired IT direction.

The amount of resource required is not easily determined. In Chapter 9, I described how quality, cost, schedule and scope are all interrelated, and that applies to overall IT direction as well as it does to an individual project. As a general rule, a given set of IT objectives will take longer to achieve if less resource is used to achieve them. But there are minimums and maximums to apply to the equation as well. Resource below a certain level won't even be able to maintain your existing infrastructure, much less make any progress toward your objectives. On the other hand, too much resource will actually cause delays due to the confusion of managing too many people.

Secret 41: Achieve your IT objectives faster by focusing on what's truly important. Focus includes preventing work on things that aren't relevant or productive.

The biggest single factor that influences your rate of progress toward achieving your IT objectives is the ability of your company to focus on what's truly important. If all of your resources above the base infrastructure maintenance level are devoted to achieving your objectives, then success will come much faster than if resource is wasted on non-critical projects. I'll emphasize again that a key part of leadership is preventing work on things which aren't relevant or productive.

Improving Efficiency

Efficiency is the way you do things — not the things you do. So an organization with an efficiency problem may be doing the right things and heading in the right direction, but they're failing to execute as well as we would like.

Secret 42: To increase the efficiency of an IT organization, optimize people, processes, and tools.

Let's start with people. For people to be most efficient, they need the right aptitudes and skills for their jobs. They need to be properly motivated to want to do their jobs. And they need to have obstacles removed from their path.

The hiring process can ensure that people with the right aptitudes are selected, but skills are a function of training and practice. Motivation comes partly from hiring (selecting people who want to do the work that's needed) and partly from the leadership of an organization (see the discussion earlier in this chapter on improving effectiveness). Obstacles can be severe drains on efficiency as well as demotivators; typical obstacles can be anything from bad working conditions to unnecessary bureaucracy.

Optimizing people means that we optimize each of the factors that influence people. We determine whether we've hired the right people, we make sure they have enough training and experience, we provide leadership and motivation, and we remove the obstacles that stand in the way of their success. It sounds simple, but it's very difficult. There aren't any shortcuts for people efficiency, but here's one tip I can give you: Treat each person as an individual and try to find a way to align each individual's personal goals with the goals of the organization. If people are simultaneously achieving their own objectives and the organization's objectives, then their motivation and commitment will be much higher.

Processes are the second element in organizational efficiency. Every person has his or her own process for doing things, but standardized processes ensure that everyone is doing certain things the same way. A process can be standardized when a method of doing something is found to be superior to other methods. Here are a few keys to more efficient processes:

1. Processes should evolve as people think of ways to improve them.
2. Standardized processes should be used for some things but not for everything. The trick is knowing when a standardized process is appropriate and when it's more appropriate to let people be creative and do things their own way.
3. Even for areas for which no standardized processes have been defined, there are still best practices that can be shared so that these non-standardized processes can be improved.

4. If the resources spent on the ongoing management and admin-istration of a standardized process start to exceed the resources saved by using the process (regardless of how much money has been spent or saved in the past), then it's time to consider abandoning the standard.

Tools are the third element in organizational efficiency. IT tools are part of the IT infrastructure just like the tools used outside of the IT organization, they have to be maintained and supported by the IT organization, and so the same secrets from Chapter 3 apply. In particular, remember secrets 7 and 8: almost any IT tool will work in the short term — it's in the long term where there's a difference; and the fewer IT tools you have, the better off you'll be, as long as you've chosen good tools.

Just as a screwdriver makes us more efficient when we turn a screw, an IT tool makes a particular IT process more efficient. Tools range from network monitors which alert support people when something goes wrong, to software development tools that simplify the development of application software. To justify a tool, the value of the tool in labor savings or risk avoidance has to exceed the initial price and ongoing cost of the tool, including the cost of training for the tool users. There are many good IT tools on the market, but it's important to focus on the ones that truly provide value.

I've said that to improve IT efficiency you have to optimize people, tools and processes, but if you're not in IT then it will be hard to tell whether or not your IT organization is optimized. Many companies use benchmarks to attempt to assess their IT efficiency, comparing their own IT organizations to the IT organizations in similar companies. However, the key to successful benchmark-ing is to figure out which companies are truly similar. You can't just assume that another company in a similar business to yours with about the same revenue will have an equivalent IT need, nor can you assume that the IT organization is equally successful (or unsuccessful) in meeting that need. I once worked with a com-pany, "Company A," which attempted to compare the size of its

IT staff to another similar company, "Company B," even though Company B was PC-based and Company A had both PC's and Macs, Company A outsourced some of its support while Company B did everything in-house, and Company B was considerably more advanced in the use of IT for some of its basic company processes. The analysis was interesting, but no value could be gained from any number comparisons.

Your best bet in improving IT efficiency is to do three things:

1. Figure out a few measurements of IT efficiency that have a relationship to business benefit, and strive for improvement in those measurements.
2. Push people in your IT organization to do their own benchmarking against other companies and organizations, not just as a way of measuring, but as a way of learning about best practices that can be used to improve your IT processes.
3. Have your IT organization bring in an occasional consultant to make specific recommendations for improvement. Or, for less money, create a culture within the IT organization that encourages and rewards people for improving efficiency.

Taking Advantage of Wind Direction

A couple of times in this book I've compared IT to a ship, mostly to stress the need for a destination and a compass. Now let me take the analogy farther. IT is actually more like a sailing ship than a craft powered by an engine. A sailing ship doesn't just head straight for its destination. Instead, it has to take the prevailing winds into account, and it has to tack back and forth to take maximum advantage of the wind.

I'm a firm believer in the need for every company to have an IT strategy, and I described the process for creating such a strategy in Chapter 8. But in most companies, IT is not the most important thing going on in the company, and I don't want you to get the impression that the IT strategy drives the company. Instead, the reverse is true; the company drives the IT strategy. There will be objectives within the IT organization that relate directly to business goals, and those objectives will probably be achieved as fast as possible. But there will be other objectives within the IT organization that are important to the long-term effectiveness and efficiency of IT, but which don't easily relate directly to specific business objectives. For example, every company wants reliable systems, but making your existing systems more reliable usually isn't a company-level business priority unless you've suffered some significant recent loss due to system problems. Other examples might be the consolidation of data centers or the replacement of an adequate but aging software product.

For IT objectives like these, which are important but not critical, the sailing ship analogy applies.

Secret 43: To achieve IT objectives which are important but not critical, take advantage of your company's "wind direction."

Rather than to go after these objectives directly, you might have to define some intermediate steps along the way, and tie the accomplishment of these intermediate steps to other more business-critical projects that they support. In effect, you are "tacking" the long-term project back and forth to take advantage of the winds: the current business projects that support your intermediate steps.

And just as a sailing ship has to sail a longer distance to reach its destination because of the tacking, you'll find that sometimes the achievement of a long-term IT objective will involve some steps that might seem a little bit off the route. But that's the price to pay for achieving the best compromise between business objectives and technology objectives. And the ultimate measure is whether you can achieve both sets of objectives simultaneously.

Exercises — Making IT Personal

1. How well does your IT organization do the "mechanic" part of IT? What could they do better?

2. Who does the "driver" part of IT in your company? Is it the IT organization or someone else? Who, if anyone, has the explicit responsibility for the "driver" part? How well do they do it? How should it be changed?

3. Is your IT organization as effective as it should be? What are you going to do to increase its effectiveness?

4. Is your IT organization as efficient as it should be? What are you going to do to increase its efficiency?

5. What are some examples of your company's IT objectives that aren't tied to company-level business priorities? How can you "take advantage of wind direction" by tying these objectives to intermediate steps of business-critical projects that they support?

Chapter 17: Putting It All Together

There's been a huge amount of change in Information Technology over the last thirty years. Batch processing has given way to online systems. Low capacity magnetic tape has been replaced by disks with incredible capacity. Mainframes have given way to minicomputers, which have been mostly replaced with personal computers and servers. Centralized systems have been decentralized and then in some cases centralized again. Dumb terminals have been replaced with client/server systems which have now mostly been replaced with web-based systems (which look a lot like the dumb terminal systems). Low-speed wired networks have been replaced with extremely-high-speed wired and wireless networks. We've gone from proprietary networks in every company to an Internet that's shared across the world.

Obviously in one sense IT people are good at some types of change — they've certainly adapted to a lot of technology change over these years. But, as I pointed out in Chapters 13 and 16, IT people are less skilled at helping the *business* to change.

There are a number of parallels between buildings and Information Technology; I've referenced a few of them in other parts of this book. When you start from scratch on a new building, you usually have an architect work with you to get an understanding of what you want. The architect gathers technical data like the number of square feet needed and the types of activities that will take place in the building. But the architect goes beyond gathering that basic information to get a sense for the "feeling" that the building should convey to its occupants and to people who see it from the outside. This feeling associated with the building is difficult to describe with common building terms. It requires more poetic language, with words like airy, ethereal, substantial, unyielding, impregnable, contemplative, whimsical, conservative, or erudite.

The design of processes and systems has similarities to the design of buildings. There is a matter-of-fact statistical part of the process (e.g., how many transactions per day do we have to process? How many simultaneous users?), but there are also intangible aspects of process and system design that relate to the feeling a person gets from using a system. If the system is used only occasionally then we might want it to be fun to use. If the system is used constantly with a high volume of keyboard input activity, then we might want the system to be fast, sleek and robust.

There is an art to designing any device or structure used by human beings, and this art is applicable to information systems and processes as well. People with these artistic skills are frequently missing in small IT organizations, just as you don't usually employ a building architect to design a tool shed. There is an assumption that small IT organizations don't need architecture. This assumption is probably correct if you intend to throw away all of your systems when your company gets bigger. But if that's not your assumption, then you'd better think about architecture from the start.

Secret 44: We wouldn't be where we are if we'd planned it; but now that we're here, we don't have to stay.

As the needs of a company grow, and as the IT organization grows, the need for architecture and "city planning" (see Chapter 8) sneaks up on us. There's an myth about boiling a frog that illustrates the problem. According to the myth, if you want to cook a live frog and you put him in boiling water, he'll hop out; but if you put him in cold water and gradually heat the water, the frog will slowly adjust to the increasing water temperature and will remain in the pot until cooked. The myth is often used by change agents to illustrate how companies and processes go through gradual change to reach a point that they would never accept if they were to move directly toward that point. And that's exactly what has happened to Information Technology.

No one in Information Technology ever started out with the goal of confusing people about information systems, but the people who are attracted to working with computers aren't usually the best at communicating with human beings. Company complexity, process complexity, and a legacy of people who "can't live without XYZ" have all contributed to a nightmarish technology monster that has almost taken on a life of its own. The IT people are overwhelmed with the care and feeding of the monster, but in most cases they're unable to satisfactorily communicate their issues to the business users. As a result, many business users have accepted "computer problems" as a way of life. Blaming the computer — or its representative, the IT organization — has become a national pastime, and is now as much of a cliché as "the check is in the mail." Software and hardware vendors exacerbate the problem by creating a steady stream of "enhanced" technology, and then using their considerable marketing budgets to convince people that the technology is required, usually before the technology is mature enough for day-to-day use (hence the Hype Cycle described in Chapter 1).

By now you should realize that when IT is not working well in a company, it's usually a victim of its own circumstances. There are some incredibly bright people in IT, but because most of their skills and capabilities have been focused on the "how," some of these skills and capabilities haven't been put to optimum use for the business. Add communication difficulties and some "magic" (which increases the size of the wall between IT and the rest of the business) and you get the current state of Information Technology: still in the driver-as-mechanic stage and not yet mature enough to be hidden "under the hood."

How do we get out of this situation? By encouraging communication between IT organizations and their customers on real business issues, and by refusing to let business people blame the IT organization for business problems that are caused by poor communication. OK, so maybe the IT people are more focused on the "how" then they ought to be. But let's build on strengths rather than belittle personal weaknesses. Where IT organizations aren't communicating properly, let's provide them with help so that the required communication can take place anyway.

Things in IT are much more complex than they have to be, but a few long-standing myths have stood in the way of making things better. I wrote this book to shatter those myths, create active communication between business people and IT people, and thereby enable the reader to improve IT effectiveness.

The secrets of IT are out, and to the reader of this book, Information Technology organizations no longer have anything to hide. Start the communication flow, force yourself to deal with IT issues instead of just blaming the IT people, and we'll begin to move forward into the next era of totally useful information technology.

I started Chapter 1 with a quotation, so it's only fitting that I end the book with one as well. I think Albert Einstein summed it up nicely when he said, "Everything should be made as simple as possible, but not one bit simpler."

Exercises — Making IT Personal

1. Go back to the lists you made doing the exercises for this book's introduction. What have you learned from this book that will help you deal with any issues or misunderstandings you're

having with your current IT organization? What have you learned to help you improve your company's use of IT?

Endnotes

Chapter 1: Poof, There It is!

The Arthur C. Clarke quotation is from the book *Profiles of the Future*, originally published in 1962, and revised in 1973. The quotation is known as Clarke's Third Law, and was added in the revised version.

Gregory Benford, a science fiction author and physicist on the faculty of the University of California, Irvine, has proposed a corollary to Clarke's Third Law, "Any technology distinguishable from magic is insufficiently advanced." I disagree with the corollary — understanding a technology (or at least a simple outer layer) is what makes it usable.

Chapter 2: In IT We Trust?

I offer my apologies to any medical doctors who are offended by my comparison between IT people and doctors. Doctors get a fair amount of respect, but they deserve even more.

For some interesting perspective on trust, I recommend *The Five Dysfunctions of a Team* by Patrick M. Lencioni. It's an eye-opening book that you can use to make your teams or your organizations work better together.

Chapter 3: The Stuff Inside Your Walls

The airline magazine phenomenon is well known in the IT industry. I've seen IT people cringe when they hear about one of their executives making a long trip because they know that the person is going to come back from the trip with a bunch of simplistic ideas that are supposed to "revolutionize" the company. Of course, in the last few years the trend has been more toward the "saw it on the Internet" phenomenon.

Chapter 4: Keeping the Pipes Clean

I used three terms in Secret 11 — "middleware," "integration broker," and "web services" — because the terminology in this area is evolving rapidly, and I wanted to make sure that at least one of the terms is still in use at the time you read this book. That's another one of the problems in Information Technology; even the people who work with it on a day-to-day basis have to keep up-to-date on the latest terminology, or they won't be able to converse with one another.

Chapter 5: Think of a Number Between 1 and 1,000

I've avoided war stories in this chapter, but I've certainly seen a lot of mistakes made.

Chapter 6: You Want It WHEN?

For more information on the Standish Group, see http://www.standishgroup.com.

Here are some of my favorite books on project management:

- *Waltzing with Bears: Managing Risk on Software Projects* by Tom DeMarco & Timothy Lister
- *Critical Chain*, a "business novel" by Eliyahu M. Goldratt
- *The Mythical Man-Month* by Frederick P. Brooks, Jr.
- *Peopleware: Productive Projects and Teams* by Tom DeMarco & Timothy Lister

And see http://www.makingITclear.com/pages/resources.html for additional useful resources,

Chapter 7: It's Not Just Like Tuning Up the Car

I am not the first person to observe that the use of the word "maintenance" in conjunction with software is totally different from our normal use of the word. I would offer credit where credit is due, but I heard this observation so long ago that I can't recall the original source.

Chapter 8: Are We There Yet?

See the www.makingITclear.com web site for more information on IT strategy.

For a list of six IT strategy decisions that often get made by default due to a lack of an integrated business/IT strategy, see the article "Six IT Decisions Your IT People Shouldn't Make" in the November, 2002 issue of *Harvard Business Review*.

You might also be interested in reading "IT Doesn't Matter," an article in the May, 2003 issue of *Harvard Business Review* in which the author, Nicholas G. Carr, makes the case that IT is no longer strategic because all companies have equal access to it. Carr believes that instead of investing in strategic IT, companies should spend less, follow others, and "focus on vulnerabilities, not opportunities." Of course, even if you follow this direction, you still need an IT strategy.

Chapter 9: Can Nine Women Have a Baby in a Month?

I invented the QCSS acronym myself as a way of remembering "Quality, Cost, Schedule, Scope," so don't expect to see it used elsewhere.

The idea for using the human gestation period as an example of non-linearity originally came from Frederick P. Brooks Jr., in his book *The Mythical Man-Month.*

Chapter 10: How'd We Get into this Mess?

I make the statement that "The systems are typically linked together by primary data flows, and within each system there are databases which store the data used by the individual system." However, just as highways are more efficient at moving traffic between areas of people, middleware is more efficient at moving data between systems. See Secret 11 in my description of Infrastructure in Chapter 4.

Chapter 11: Simple, Simpler, Simplest

For a wonderful book on the subject of the 80-20 Rule, see *The 80/20 Principle: The Secret of Achieving More with Less* by Richard Koch.

Chapter 12: YOUR System was Bad Today

Thanks to Bob Keefe, CIO for Russell Corporation, for recognizing that this topic needed to be included in the book, and to John Mullin, Associate Vice President and Associate Vice Provost for Information Technology at Georgia Tech, for reminding me of the "*your* system" problem.

Chapter 13: Parlez vous Anglais?

Again, I offer my apologies to any medical doctors who are offended by my comparison between IT people and doctors. And for this chapter I guess I ought to apologize to IT people as well. My observations in this chapter are necessarily general, and I readily admit that there are exceptions. Some IT people are *very* focused on the *what*; I just wish there were more of them.

Chapter 14: Sprechen sie Business?

If the explanation for Secret 37 seems familiar, you may have seen a slightly different version in the November, 2004 MakingITclear® Newsletter under the title "Use their terminology – not yours". I have also distributed the same article through EzineArticles.com so you may have seen it on other Internet web sites.

Chapter 15: Have Your "Guy" Do It

There's another variation on outsourcing that I haven't discussed: "spinning off" a part of your organization as a separate company. The theory is that this makes the group more responsive to business needs, and it allows the group to take advantage of economies of scale by adding other customers to build revenue mass. But I've never seen it done successfully; the spun-off organization has to add a lot of business infrastructure to compete in the real world, and this almost invariably leads to economic failure.

What *can* be done successfully, however, is to outsource a part of your organization, and then have the outsourcing company hire some of your displaced employees. This gives you the advantages (and disadvantages) of outsourcing without some of the layoffs.

Chapter 16: Who's the Designated Driver?

For still more on improving IT effectiveness, including a free monthly e-mail newsletter, go to http://www.makingITclear.com.

Chapter 17: Putting It All Together

For an article disproving the "boiling the frog" myth, see the November, 1995 issue of *Fast Company* magazine. No frogs were harmed in the creation of this book.

Acknowledgements

As any author knows, a book only comes at the end of a long journey. First comes the background knowledge that makes the book possible. For this I'm indebted to many people, but in particular to my faculty advisor at MIT, Professor Thomas J. Allen, who first opened my eyes to the more human aspects of management.

Once I left school and joined the real world, I had a succession of role models to emulate. I've worked with some incredible people over the years, including Bob Lynch, Dave Ehrman, Jack Wuenschel and Bart Bolton at Digital Equipment Corporation; and Harry Benjamin and Rick King at Ceridian Corporation. I've also been heavily influenced by a few authors who gave me a new perspective on IT, including Gerald Weinberg, Frederick P. Brooks Jr., and Ed Yourdon.

Everyone has negative role models as well – sometimes it's easier to learn when you have an example of how *not* to do things. I've certainly had my share of negative role models, but I'll express my appreciation to them silently, leaving their names out of this book in the hope that they've learned a few things since I knew them.

Any book starts with an idea, and the idea for this book came to me when I was first asked to speak to Executive MBA students by Rich Daniels, the Director of the Executive MBA Program for the Terry College of Business at the University of Georgia. Although the material in this book has evolved and grown a great deal from my original 2003 presentation, I'm indebted to Terry College for launching me down this path.

Once an early draft of a manuscript is created, it's important to get real-world feedback to make sure the author is communicating clearly and to keep potential ranting under control. Three people went through the manuscript in detail and gave me their feedback: Bill Hauserman, Bob Keefe, and Sandy Hofmann. I'm very grateful for the help these people gave me. However, I went against their comments and advice in a few areas, so if you find fault with this book, blame me – not them.

To turn a manuscript into a book requires a publisher, and to get a publisher normally requires an agent. I was very fortunate to find Faith Hamlin at Sanford J. Greenburger Associates in New York. She believed in my work when few others would, and I thank her for her efforts. Ultimately, however, even Ms. Hamlin was unable to convince the traditional publishing houses to take on my book. Maybe it's because my book topic falls into the gap between two categories; it talks about IT, which is a technical subject, but it does so from a business perspective. In the end, I decided to publish the book through my own company, MakingITclear, Inc., and this is the result.

I have one final acknowledgement. Although the acquisition of knowledge and perspective comes from involvement with other people, writing itself is a solitary activity, and psychological support during the writing process is critical to success. I can't say that my wife Sharon has never doubted me, but that's probably a good thing. Books are for the reader – not the author – and an author may need an encouraging skeptic more than an unconditional advocate. Sharon has certainly been my encouraging skeptic, and I appreciate her efforts and her love.

Index

Q

QCSS
 Curves can reverse 93
 Defined 91
 Home construction example 92
 House painter example 93
 Non-linearity 92
 Recommendations for projects 95
 Violations 95
 Where the acronym came from 168
Quality Improvement 149
Quality related to Cost, Schedule and
  Scope 91

R

Rank, in the buying decision 29
Reason vs. excuse 42
Requirements
 Car example 64
 Gathering vs. Negotiating 64
 Overly-specific 20, 131
 Pushing back against 131
Reservation desk 8
Resources 152
Return on Investment (ROI) 48
 How to improve 53
 Why it isn't working 52
Rework
 As part of a project 60
Risk
 Infrastructure 25
 Project 61

Road map
 As part of IT strategy 86
ROI. *See* Return on Investment (ROI)
Role Models 171
Roles and Responsibilities 117
 As a barrier to effectiveness 150
Russell Corporation 169

S

Sales Management System (SMS)
  40
Sanders, Barbara 136
SAP 41, 43, 86
Schedule, related to Quality, Cost and
  Scope 91
Scope, related to Quality, Cost and
  Schedule 91
Secretary example in ROI 49
Ship
 Comparing IT to a 73, 74, 88, 149,
  156
Simplicity 107
 Simplifying systems 103
 Why isn't IT simple? 97
Six IT Decisions Your IT People
  Shouldn't Make 167
Skills 154
Slack time 62
Software
 Choosing the right software 26
 Cost of fixing mistakes 60
 Current versions 37
 Evolutionary forces 102

X

Y

About the Author

Harwell Thrasher is an author, speaker and advisor specializing in the human side of Information Technology. Harwell shows IT and business people how to work together more effectively by taking the magic out of IT. He sometimes describes himself as a "jiggler" because he helps unstick companies and IT organizations who are stuck in their old ways of doing things.

Harwell founded MakingITclear, Inc. in 2002 after more than thirty years of experience working in and around IT organizations. Of all the work he did during those thirty years, Harwell is most proud of:

- Performing technology due diligence for over twenty acquisitions in the U.S., Canada, the U.K., and Switzerland, and helping the acquired companies integrate their IT strategies with the strategy of the acquiring company
- Totally revamping the systems and processes for a financial services business, allowing it to handle three times the volume without adding any more people
- Creating an Internet payroll product
- Developing and managing Material Requirements Planning systems for manufacturing plants around the world

A graduate of MIT's Sloan School of Management, Harwell is an Atlanta native.

Made in the USA